Start Bridge the Easy Way

The enormous success of the TV bridge programmes confirms the rapidly growing interest among many people who have never played the game. This book by Hugh Kelsey, one of the world's leading bridge writers, provides an ideal introduction for those who want to start under the best guidance.

Hugh Kelsey starts from the basics – a table, four chairs and two packs of cards – and takes the beginner gently through the objectives of the game into bidding and play. All the beginner needs to know about bidding and the responses, how to read your opponents' bids, what cards to lead when opening the play as well as the general principles of card play are carefully covered. And if you are lucky enough to find yourself with a potential slam hand you will know how to bid and make it.

Start Bridge the Easy Way was originally published in a hardbound edition under the title of *Learn Bridge for Fun*.

Start Bridge the Easy Way

HUGH KELSEY

LONDON
VICTOR GOLLANCZ LTD
in association with Peter Crawley
1983

© Hugh Kelsey 1976

First published in 1976 by
Ward Lock Limited under
the title *Learn Bridge for Fun*

British Library Cataloguing in Publication Data
Kelsey, H.W.
   [Learn bridge for fun.] Start bridge the
  easy way.
  1. Contract bridge
  I. Title   II. Start bridge the easy way.
  795.41′5   GV1281.3

  ISBN 0-575-03254-5

Printed in Great Britain
at The Camelot Press Ltd, Southampton

Contents

Acknowledgments

I am grateful to George Jesner
for making a careful and critical survey of my draft.
Many of his suggestions have been adopted
in the final text.

H.K.

Introduction

Does your mind ever boggle? Mine does when I reflect that some people manage to get through a lifetime without once playing a game of bridge. What a lot of pleasure they deny themselves.

The reasons for the rise in popularity of contract bridge, from its inception in 1925 to its present unchallenged position as the most widely-played game of all time, are numerous. Bridge has something for everyone. The extrovert accepts it as a ready-made vehicle for the expression of his personality, while the introvert finds that the game opens a painless door to a wide range of social contacts and friendships. Educationalists see bridge as offering a valuable mental discipline, encouraging desirable traits, such as courtesy and forbearance, and punishing undesirable ones, such as selfishness and greed. Yet the game is not entirely a moral exercise, for it appeals strongly to the competitive instinct—that atavistic urge that lurks in all of us to get the better of the other fellow. As an intellectual challenge bridge is unsurpassed, the higher reaches of the game affording glimpses of metaphysical beauties undreamed of by the non-player.

But the main reason why so many people play bridge is, of course, for the sheer enjoyment of it. With three agreeable companions and a pack of cards, a player can escape from the cares of everyday life and spend a few hours utterly absorbed in the pleasures of the game. A feature that appeals particularly to the beginner is the happy way in which luck and skill are interwoven in the fabric of the game. In the long run skill must prevail, but luck plays a big part in the short term and is responsible for those magic moments when the beginner gets the better of the expert.

If you have not yet tried bridge, it may be because you lack the confidence to make a start. The remedy lies in your hands. This book is your passport to an exciting new world. It is designed to help you over the initial hurdles and point you firmly in the right direction. Between these covers you will find all you need to enable you to take your place at the bridge table without fear of spoiling the game for your friends.

I suggest that you first read quickly through the book from beginning to end, skipping over any points that puzzle you. This will give you some idea of what the game is all about, and you will discover that everything will fall into place when you go back for a second reading. This time take it chapter by chapter and try to grasp the principles involved. Ideally, you should supplement your reading with a little practice in the company of friends who are also beginners.

If you are still with me at the end of the second reading, you will have acquired a hobby to last a lifetime and an endless source of delight.

1. Making a Start

Bridge is a game for four, in which partners sit opposite one another with opponents to right and left. The game is played with an ordinary pack of cards from which the jokers have been removed. There are those who would like to remove jokers from amongst the players as well, but most of us insist on enjoying our bridge.

The Pack

The fifty-two cards in the pack are made up of thirteen cards in each of four suits. The suits are ♠ spades, ♡ hearts, ◇ diamonds and ♣ clubs. The cards in each suit rank from the ace (highest), king, queen, jack (or knave, as it is sometimes called), ten, and so on down to the two (lowest).

Tricks

In the play of the cards the objective is to win tricks. Each player in clockwise rotation places a card from his hand face upwards on the table. These four cards constitute a trick, which is won by the player who contributes the highest card of the suit led. There is an obligation on all players to 'follow suit'. This means that if the first player leads a spade, for instance, each of the other players must play a spade if he has one in his hand. Having no spades, a player may play any card he chooses.

Let us have a look at a diagram.

5 of hearts

king of hearts 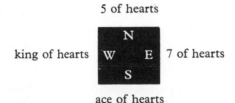 7 of hearts

ace of hearts

In bridge diagrams it is convenient to use the cardinal points of the compass to designate the players. North and South are partners against East and West.

West leads the king of hearts, North plays the five, East the seven and South the ace of hearts. The ace being the highest card, South wins the trick. He gathers the four cards and places them face downwards in a neat pile in front of him. Winning a trick gives a player the privilege of leading to the next trick, so in this case it is up to South to make the next lead.

Each player begins with thirteen cards, and it follows that there are thirteen tricks to be won on every hand. The art of card play lies in exploiting the potential of the partnership cards so as to win as many of the thirteen tricks as possible.

Trumps

The highest card of the suit led will not always win the trick, for there may be a trump suit. This is any one of the four suits which, in that particular hand, has precedence over the other suits. The trump suit is determined by the auction, as we shall see shortly, and it is a fact that a trump suit is present in most bridge hands.

The next diagram illustrates the sort of thing that can happen when there is a trump suit. Assume that diamonds are trumps.

king of spades

jack of spades   N   W   E   ace of spades

S

3 of diamonds (trumps)

West leads the jack of spades, North covers with the king and East plays the ace, expecting to win the trick. But South has no spades and is able to play a small trump. The lowly three of diamonds wins the trick, and East reacts with a wry smile or an explosive oath according to his nature.

Cutting for Partners

Let us go back for a moment to see exactly what happens when four players sit down at the bridge table. In the absence of any pre-arrangement it is customary to cut for partners. The pack is spread out face downwards on the table and each player draws a card. The players drawing the two highest cards play as partners against the other two. In the event of two players drawing cards of equal value, the ranking order of the suits decides the issue (spades rank highest, followed by hearts, diamonds and clubs).

The player who draws the highest card becomes the dealer and is entitled to two small privileges. He has the choice of seats (invaluable for those susceptible to draughts or superstitions), and also the choice of cards (it is convenient to play with two packs, although only one is used at a time).

Shuffle and Deal

The player on the dealer's left shuffles the cards and passes them face downwards to his partner, who 'cuts' by taking a block of cards from the top of the pack and placing them closer to the dealer. The dealer

10

completes the cut by bringing the cards originally at the bottom of the pack to the top. He then deals out all the cards one at a time, starting with the player on his left, continuing in a clockwise direction and finishing with himself. Meanwhile his partner shuffles the other pack and places it on his right, ready for the next deal. This saves a little time between deals, and you will soon discover that keen players grudge every second wasted on routine matters, such as shuffling and dealing, when they could be bidding and playing.

When the deal is completed, the players pick up their cards and sort them into suits, taking care not to show their hands to the other players. Then the fun begins.

The Auction

The dealer has the right to make the first bid. With a weak hand he may elect to pass by saying 'No bid', but with a strong hand he will certainly make a bid of some kind.

A bid at bridge is an undertaking to win a stated number of tricks above six, either with a specified trump suit or with no trumps. Thus a bid of one club is an offer to make seven tricks with clubs as trumps, a bid of two hearts promises to take eight tricks with hearts as trumps, and a bid of three no trumps is a contract to take nine tricks without any trump suit.

As in any auction, the early bids are generally made at a low level. When the dealer has bid or passed, it is the turn of the player on his left (all the action at the bridge table takes place in a clockwise direction). Each player in turn is entitled to bid, and the auction continues until no one is prepared to go any higher. The only rule is that each bid must be an advance on the previous bid. It must contract either for more tricks or for the same number of tricks in a higher denomination. The ranking table reads as follows:

No trumps
Spades
Hearts
Diamonds
Clubs

The suits are in reverse alphabetical order, with no trumps outranking them all. Thus after a bid of one heart you may bid one spade or one no trump, but if you wish to bid clubs or diamonds you must go to the two-level.

At times one pair or the other will hold most of the high cards, making the auction a one-sided affair. When the strength is more evenly divided, the auction may be contested, with each side competing keenly for the right to nominate trumps and play the hand. In all cases the auction is terminated by three successive passes.

Here is an example of a competitive auction.

SOUTH	WEST	NORTH	EAST
1 ♠	2 ◇	no bid	3 ◇
3 ♡	4 ◇	4 ♡	no bid
no bid	no bid		

South, the dealer, opens with a bid of one spade, which, as we have seen, is a promise to win seven tricks with spades as trumps. The auction seldom dies at such a low level, however. West, who is next to speak, has a diamond suit, which he feels is worth a mention. He cannot bid one diamond, for that would be a lower call than one spade, so he makes the cheapest legitimate bid in his suit by saying two diamonds.

North passes, having a weak hand without support for spades, but East finds the strength to raise his partner to three diamonds. South has a strong hand and has not finished yet. He introduces another suit by bidding three hearts. He can bid at the three-level since hearts rank higher than diamonds. West competes further with a bid of four diamonds, and North comes to life by bidding four hearts. No one has any more to say and four hearts becomes the final contract. North and South have undertaken to win ten tricks out of the thirteen with hearts as trumps.

The player who first names the suit of the final contract is called the declarer and has the task of playing both his own cards and his partner's cards. Thus although North made the final bid of four hearts, South becomes the declarer, because he was the first to mention the suit. The opponents become the defenders, whose objective will be to defeat the contract of four hearts by winning at least four tricks themselves.

The Play

When the auction has ended, it is up to the defender on the left of the declarer to start the play. He makes the opening lead by placing one of his cards face upwards on the table.

As soon as the opening lead has been made, the declarer's partner lays all his cards face upwards on the table. He should sort them neatly into suits, placing the trumps (if any) on his right. This is called the dummy hand. The declarer's partner, who is also referred to as dummy, may take no active part in the play of the cards. It is up to the declarer to attempt to fulfil his contract by playing the cards from both hands (in proper clockwise rotation, of course).

Scoring

We are not going to dwell on this at any great length, for scoring is a dull subject and one that is best learned by experience. A full scoring table is given on page 96, but there are some basic features that you need to know from the start.

First, let us see what a score-pad looks like.

The vertical line down the middle separates the scores of the goodies from the baddies. The heavy horizontal line divides bonus points from trick points.

WE	THEY

A rubber at bridge is the best of three games, and to make a game you need to score 100 points below the horizontal line. These points can be scored only by bidding and making contracts. Every time you succeed in a contract you score points for each trick (over six) that you make. The awards are as follows:

No trumps	The first trick above six is worth 40 points and each subsequent trick is worth 30.
Spades and hearts (known as the major suits)	Each trick above six is worth 30 points.
Diamonds and clubs (the minor suits)	Each trick above six is worth 20 points.

The 100 points needed for game can be achieved on a single hand by bidding and making three no trumps (40+30+30), four spades or four hearts (4 x 30), or five diamonds or five clubs (5 x 20).

Game may also be reached in stages, however. Suppose you play in a contract of two diamonds and make nine tricks. That scores 40 towards game for two diamonds bid and made. The extra trick you made is worth a further 20 points, but that is scored above the line and does not count towards game. Only those tricks that are *contracted for* and made are scored below the line.

Your 40 points below the line are known as a part-score. A further 60 points are needed for game, and you may well succeed in making up the balance on a later hand. If the opponents score a game in the meanwhile, however, the value of your part-score is ended. A line is drawn right across the pad below the trick scores, and both sides start from scratch towards the next game.

Rubber Bonus

The pair that wins the rubber earns a big bonus, 700 points for a win by two games to nil and 500 for a win by two games to one.

Penalty Points

Just as there are rewards for making a contract so are there penalties for failure. Points are scored above the line by the defending side when they defeat a contract. The award is 50 points for each trick by which the contract fails if the declaring side has yet to make a game, and 100 points per trick if the declaring side has already scored a game.

Because of the heavier penalties that may be incurred, players who have scored a game are said to be vulnerable.

Double and Redouble

These are features of the auction that need a few words of explanation. If a player considers that his opponents have bitten off more than they can chew, he may say 'double' when it is his turn to bid. The effect, if the contract fails, is to increase the penalty substantially, particularly when the declarer is vulnerable. When you are vulnerable, therefore, do not stick out your neck too far in the bidding. An opponent may wield the axe.

If a contract succeeds in spite of a double, the trick score is doubled and the declarer receives a bonus of 50 points above the line. A contract of two hearts doubled and made, for example, would give the declarer a game, scoring 120 below the line and 50 above. Overtricks are also scored on an augmented scale. So it is clearly unwise to be too frisky with your doubles.

There is the further point that when you double, either of your opponents may redouble if he considers that the contract will be made. The redouble increases yet again the rewards of success and the penalties of failure.

Like any other call, a double or redouble ends the auction when it is followed by three passes. A further bid by one of the three players, however, has the effect of cancelling the double (or redouble) and keeping the auction alive.

Honours

The ace, king, queen, jack and ten are known as honour cards. If a player holds all five trump honours in one hand, he is entitled to a bonus of 150 points above the line. Four trump honours in the one hand are worth 100 points. And, in a no trump contract only, all four aces in the one hand score a bonus of 150. The proper time to claim these bonuses is at the end of the play of the hand.

Slams

A contract for twelve tricks is known as a small slam, and a contract for all thirteen tricks as a grand slam. Successful slams are rewarded by big bonuses, but I recommend a cautious approach. There is little margin for error when you contract to win twelve or thirteen tricks. That great showman of bridge, Ely Culbertson, once remarked that the players of his acquaintance would be better off if they bid no slams at all. And he was talking about experts.

Settling Up

At the end of the rubber the scores on either side, both above and below the line, are totted up and the difference calculated to the nearest hundred. Before starting the next rubber, the losers pay the winners the agreed stake multiplied by the number of hundreds in the winning margin and try to look cheerful about it.

Bridge is best played for some stake, even if it is only a tiny one, in order to keep the game sensible. In the absence of a stake a whimsical opponent may bid up to seven no trumps on every deal just to have the fun of playing the hand. You can bear it with more fortitude if he is paying for his fun.

2. Opening the Bidding

We have seen that the purpose of bidding is to arrive at a contract that suits the combined values of the partnership hands. As information is exchanged, the partners gradually build up a picture of each other's hand to the point where one of them is able to determine the best contract.

This process starts with the opening bid. The lowest bid you can make is an undertaking to win more than half of the thirteen tricks, and it follows that you need a hand that is better than average to open the bidding. But what is an average hand?

Point Count

For the purpose of valuing the high cards in your hand a simple point count is used.

Ace   = 4 points
King = 3 points
Queen = 2 points
Jack = 1 point

This gives a total of ten points in each suit, 40 in the whole pack, and 10 in an average hand.

Remember that these points are counted solely as a bidding aid. They have nothing to do with the scoring points mentioned in the last chapter.

Distribution

The strength of a bridge hand does not rest entirely upon high cards, however. The way in which the cards are divided between the suits is also important. Let us look at some examples.

a) ♠: Q 9 4   b) ♠: 6
   ♡: A 7 6 4   ♡: A K 8 7 6 3
   ◇: J 5 2   ◇: K J 4
   ♣: K Q 6   ♣: 8 3 2

Hand (a) has a total of 12 points and hand (b) only 11, yet (b) is the stronger hand because of the latent trick-taking potential of the small cards in the long suit.

This may be seen more clearly if we set out the heart suit for example (b) as it is likely to be distributed around the table and consider what will happen in the play of the cards.

♡: 9 4

♡: J 2   W   E   ♡: Q 10 5

♡: A K 8 7 6 3

Suppose that South is playing in a heart contract. When the ace of hearts is led, West will follow with the two, North with the four and East with the five. The king of hearts will draw the jack from West, the nine from North and the ten from East. On the third round East will win with the queen, while West and North throw cards from another suit. South is left in possession of the only three remaining trumps, which represent three sure tricks.

Clearly, then, a long suit confers an advantage in the play, and this should be recognized in the bidding. Hand (b) is therefore worth an opening of one heart.

In hand (a) we have what can be described as a balanced hand, with no long suit. On this type of hand we have to rely on high cards for our tricks, and hand (a) just fails to qualify for an opening bid.

The minimum requirements for an opening bid of one in a suit are:
13 points if you have no suit longer than four cards.
12 points if you have a five-card suit.
11 points if you have a six-card suit or two five-card suits.

01326 - 313 620

2 photocopies of Birth Certificate

<u>INT.</u> 12 to 14 points or even spread.
                                     not move 5 Ace
                                        or 1 Double.

<u>open</u> 13 to 20 points. → at least <u>4 cards</u> to
                                                        call

        do not reply if less than 6.

To
<u>Reply</u> in another
respond in <u>1</u> level higher placing new <u>suit</u> → at least 4
          then   <u>6 to 18</u> points.   cards.

If. 17 to 18 points. — ~~jump~~ shift. if strong.

<u>INT.</u>   mod. hand no 4 card at level of 1
        6 to 9 occasionally 10.

Use it straight from hand if a suit ~~trap~~

Response in a new suit . but to level 2.
                              then <u>10 points</u> or more

18 ~~points~~ a jump!

                                                start
                                N.Trump 4th card

        doubling (is a bid) reply.

N.Trump hand play out your <u>long</u> suit . in ~~one~~ ~~da~~ of the

There is a good reason why you should open the bidding on any hand that contains 13 points. Experience shows that on balanced hands it normally takes a combined total of at least 25 points to produce a game either in no trumps or in a major suit. If you and your partner both pass when holding 12 points, the worst that is likely to happen is that you will miss a part-score contract — no great tragedy. But if you pass with 13 points, you may miss a game and end up with two pairs of red ears.

Which Suit to Bid

The guiding principle is to bid on length. Remember that when you bid a suit you are proposing it as trumps, and you will not have a comfortable time if the opponents have more trumps than you. Bid your longest suit, therefore, when you have more than one suit to choose from.

♠ : Q 10 7 6 2
♡ : A 7 5
◇ : A K J 3
♣ : 5

Open one spade, even though most of the high cards are in diamonds. It is length, rather than strength, that counts in selecting a trump suit.

♠ : A K 8   ♠ : A J 4 2
♡ : A Q 9 4   ♡ : K Q 6 5 2
◇ : —   ◇ : K 10 7 4
♣ : 9 8 6 5 4 3   ♣ : —

Open 1♣   Open 1♡

With two six-card or two five-card suits, open in the higher ranking one.

♠ : K Q J 6 3
♡ : Q J 7 6 5
◇ : 4
♣ : K 2

Open one spade. You can bid two hearts on the next round, and if partner prefers spades he will be able to put you back into spades without raising the level of the bidding.

When you have equal length in spades and clubs, however, it is more economical to open one club.

♠ : K 8 7 6 2
♡ : K 3
◇ : 6
♣ : A Q 8 7 3

Open one club. Then you have a convenient rebid of one spade when partner responds one diamond or one heart. If you open one spade you may be unable to show the club suit below the three-level, and your hand is not strong enough to climb so high.

Think of Your Rebid

An important point to remember about opening the bidding in a suit is that you have an obligation to bid again if partner responds in a new suit. In other words, an opening bid guarantees a rebid, and unless you take care in choosing your opening bid, you may be in trouble when it comes to finding a rebid. The choice of rebid is covered in detail in Chapter 4, but it is as well to realize from the outset that opening bids are chosen with a view to easing the rebid problem.

Choice Between Four-Card Suits

There is a useful rule of thumb to follow when you have no suit longer than four cards. Bid the suit next in rank below the shortage. In applying this rule, regard the suits as forming a circle, with spades ranking next below clubs. Spades, hearts, diamonds, clubs, spades, and so on.

♠ : K J 7 4	♠ : Q J 5
♡ : 6 2	♡ : A K J 3
◇ : A Q 5 2	◇ : 4 3
♣ : K 10 4	♣ : K 8 6 5
Open 1 ◇	Open 1 ♣

♠ : 7	♠ : Q 10 8 3
♡ : K Q 9 4	♡ : A Q J 7
◇ : A Q 6 3	◇ : 8 2
♣ : A 8 5 4	♣ : A J 5
Open 1 ♡	Open 1 ♠

A Wide Range

So far we have been looking at hands with a relatively low point count, but there are many stronger hands that are also opened with a bid of one in a suit.

♠ : 8	♠ : A K 2
♡ : K J 8 7 3	♡ : 7 6
◇ : A K Q 5	◇ : A K 9 3
♣ : A Q J	♣ : A Q 9 5
Open 1 ♡	Open 1 ◇

It is apparent that the opening bid of one in a suit has a wide range of strength. The opener may have as few as 11 points or as many as 20. Clarification has to wait until the next round of bidding.

An Awkward Hand

There is one type of hand that poses a special problem — a weak hand with balanced distribution.

♠: A 10 5
♡: 9 8 6 2
◊: K 9 4
♣: A Q 7

Here there is no suit worth bidding, but the count of 13 points makes it dangerous to pass. The least of evils is to open one club, even though you lack a fourth card in the suit. By keeping the bidding as low as possible you provide yourself with a sound rebid of one no trump over a response of one diamond or one spade. If partner responds one heart, of course, you will be happy to raise to two hearts.

Opening One No Trump

Reserve the opening bid of one no trump for stronger balanced hands with a point count of 15–17. This is an arbitrary range, as you will soon discover when you move out in bridge circles. Some players will open one no trump when holding, say, 13–15 points, others perhaps with 16–18. It is just a matter of partnership agreement.

While you are learning the game, stick to 15–17 points for your opening bids of one no trump. It is a sound range, which will keep you out of trouble.

The shape of the hand must be reasonably balanced, with no singleton (one card in a suit) and not more than one doubleton (two cards in a suit). Here are some examples.

a) ♠: K J 5   b) ♠: K 10 3
   ♡: A 8 6 5   ♡: K Q 7 5
   ◊: K Q 8   ◊: A Q 8 2
   ♣: Q 9 3   ♣: K 9

Hand (a) is a minimum and hand (b) a maximum for an opening bid of one no trump.

A five-card suit is no bar to opening one no trump if the hand is suitable in other respects.

♠: A Q
♡: K 8 7
◊: K J 9 5 3
♣: Q J 3

One no trump is by far the most descriptive bid you can make on this hand.

Unlike the opening bid of one in a suit, the opening bid of one no trump has a narrow range. Knowing that you will have no fewer than 15 and no more than 17 points, partner is in a good position to decide what the final contract should be. For this reason you do not need to consider the matter of a rebid when you open one no trump. Your first bid tells practically the whole story.

Bids that define the strength and character of a hand within narrow limits are often referred to as limit bids. Remember the name, for we shall meet more of these useful bids before long.

TIP FOR TODAY
Before opening with a bid of one in a suit,
consider what your rebid will be.

3. Responses

Knowing the opener to have more than his share of the high cards in the pack, the responder is in a good position to judge the potential of the combined hands. If he has the values for an opening bid in his own hand, for instance, he can be fairly sure that there will be a play for game (13 + 13 = 26 = game). It only remains to determine the best strain (suit or no trumps) in which to play.

Even with a fairly weak hand the responder should try to keep the bidding open. The opener may be quite strong, needing only a little help to make game. Optimism has its limits, however, and there are times when a pass is the only sensible action.

Partner opens one heart, for example, and you hold:

♠ : Q 7 5
♡ : 8 5
◇ : Q J 4 2
♣ : 9 7 6 2

You have no support for partner's suit, no good suit of your own, and only 5 points. Game is highly unlikely, and there is no sound alternative to a pass.

Responding 1 NT

The response of one no trump is made on weak, balanced hands containing between 6 and 9 points. It denies the ability to bid a four-card suit at the one-level.

♠: 10 7 6
♡: J 5 3
◇: A Q 7 3
♣: 9 8 6

With this hand, respond one no trump to an opening bid of one heart or one spade. If the opening bid is one club, however, you should show your suit by responding one diamond. On weak hands it pays to keep the bidding as low as possible.

A response of one no trump may be the right move even though you have a five-card suit.

♠: 10
♡: Q J 8 6 4
◇: K 8 3
♣: J 8 3 2

If partner opens one spade, respond one no trump rather than two hearts in order to keep the bidding low. Over one club or one diamond you would naturally respond one heart.

Like opening bids in no trumps, all responses in no trumps are limit bids, defining strength and distribution within a narrow range. Knowing what you have within a point or two, partner need not bid again if he can see no prospect of game.

Stronger NT Responses

When you have a balanced hand of 11 or 12 points, your combined count cannot be far short of the magic number of 25. Your response is a jump to two no trumps, suggesting the possibility of game to partner.

♠: A Q 4   ♠: Q 9 5
♡: K 9 3   ♡: K Q 6
◇: 10 6 3   ◇: Q 7
♣: Q 9 6 2 ♣: K 8 7 5 2

Bid two no trumps in response to an opening bid of one diamond with either of these hands. If partner has a minimum opening bid, he may pass or rebid three diamonds, which you in turn will pass. With more than a minimum partner will proceed to game.

Note that these examples contain no four-card major suit. This is no accident. With a four-card major you should respond in the suit in order to explore the possibility of a major suit game. Partner has to bid again when you respond in a new suit, remember, and you can always bid no trumps on the next round.

Balanced hands of 13–15 points qualify for a response of three no trumps. The principle of the limit bid is that you indicate the full value of your hand at once. Do not bid two no trumps when you are strong enough for three no trumps, or you may miss a game and be conspued by your partner.

♠: K 10 9   ♠: Q J 2
♡: Q 10 6   ♡: A Q 6
◇: A J 7 4   ◇: K Q 6
♣: K 7 4   ♣: J 10 5 3

Holding either of these hands, respond three no trumps to an opening bid of one in any suit.

Raising Partner's Suit

When partner opens with a bid of a major suit in which you hold four or more cards, your search for the right denomination is over before it has begun. Partner's suit must be the best spot, for you have at least eight trumps to the opponents' five which is a comfortable working majority. The only problem concerns the level at which you should play.

In supporting partner's suit the limit principle again applies — you show the full value of your hand by the level to which you raise. But the point count, accurate enough for no trumps, is less reliable when it comes to raising partner's suit. The distribution of the responder's hand is a factor that has to be taken into account. Consider the following hands.

a) ♠: A J 8 3   b) ♠: Q 10 8 5 3
    ♡: 10 5 2   ♡: 7 5 4
    ◇: K 7 4   ◇: —
    ♣: 9 8 4   ♣: 10 9 7 6 2

Hand (a) counts to 8 points and hand (b) to only 2, yet (b) may well turn out to be the stronger hand in support of partner's opening bid of one spade. The fifth trump counts for something, as does the length in clubs, but the main bull point is the void (no cards) in diamonds. The void gives you control, preventing the opponents from making any tricks in the suit. Furthermore, if partner has some small diamonds in his hand he will be able to make extra tricks by trumping them in dummy.

Shortage in a side suit is a highly desirable feature when you are contemplating a raise of partner's suit. The next best thing to a void is a singleton (one card in a suit), and even a doubleton (two cards) has some value. The better the distribution, the fewer points are needed for a single raise. Hands (a) and (b) above are both worth a raise to two spades.

Here are some more typical raises.

♠: 8	♠: J 5
♡: K 10 9 2	♡: 9 8 5 2
◇: Q 6 5 2	◇: A Q 7
♣: 8 6 3 2	♣: J 8 7 2

Raise an opening bid of one heart to two hearts on either of these hands.

At a pinch you may raise partner's major suit with only three-card support, but your trumps should be headed by an honour card and the hand should not be too weak.

♠: Q J 6	♠: K 7 4
♡: 10 6 5 3	♡: 3
◇: A 9 8 5	◇: K 9 5 4
♣: 7 2	♣: Q 7 5 3 2

Raise an opening bid of one spade to two spades on either hand.

A single raise normally indicates from 6 to 9 points, but remember that some points can be dispensed with when you have four or more trumps and good distribution.

Stronger Raises

With a stronger hand in support of partner's major suit you can invite game by giving a double raise. That is a raise of one spade to three spades, or one heart to three hearts. Partner may pass if he has opened on a minimum hand, but he will otherwise proceed to game.

This double raise is never made with fewer than four trumps. The normal standard is 11–12 points, but this may be shaded down to about 9 if the distribution is particularly good.

♠: A J 7 3	♠: K Q 9 5
♡: 4 2	♡: 5
◇: K J 8 4	◇: A 10 9 7 3
♣: Q J 2	♣: 8 7 6

Raise one spade to three spades with either of these hands.

When you have a still stronger hand containing 13–15 points (or 11–12 and exceptional distribution), raise directly to game with four or more cards in partner's major suit.

♠: K Q 4	♠: 5 2
♡: Q 10 8 3	♡: K Q 7 3 2
◇: J 3	◇: A Q 8 7 5
♣: A Q 6 2	♣: 3

Raise one heart to four hearts with either hand.

Raising a Minor Suit

There is not the same incentive to raise when partner bids a minor suit. Game in a minor, requiring eleven tricks, is rather a distant prospect and will normally require a combined point count of 28 or more. You should prefer to respond in a major suit when you have one. Partner may be able to support your major or to bid no trumps, and you will generally find nine or ten tricks an easier target than eleven.

Nevertheless, there are hands on which there is no sound alternative to raising a minor suit. Suppose partner opens one diamond and you hold:

a) ♠: 8 4 3   b) ♠: A 9 6 3
   ♡: 6 3   ♡: 6 3
   ◇: Q J 7 5   ◇: Q J 7 5
   ♣: A 9 6 3   ♣: 8 4 3

Raise to two diamonds on (a) but prefer a response of one spade on (b).

Follow the same principle with regard to double raises. Suppose partner opens one club and you hold:

c) ♠: J 8 5   d) ♠: J 8 5
   ♡: A Q J   ♡: A Q J 4
   ◇: 5 4   ◇: 5
   ♣: Q J 10 6 4 ♣: Q J 10 6 4

Raise to three clubs on (c) but explore with a response of one heart on (d).

Responding in a New Suit

We have already come across one or two examples of a response in a new suit. These responses are unlimited, in the sense that they have a wide range. You may bid a new suit at the one-level with no more than 6 points. A response in a new suit at the two-level promises rather more strength — from 8 points upwards. And with no more than 8 or 9 points you should also have a good five-card or longer suit. The top limit for a response in a new suit is in the region of 16 points.

The wide range explains why it is necessary for your partner to bid again when you respond in a new suit. A pass could lead to a missed game if your hand is in the upper range. In the language of bridge a response in a new suit is said to be 'forcing for one round'. Opener is obliged to bid at least once more.

Note that a limit bid — a response in no trumps or a raise of partner's suit — will generally give a better picture of your hand. A response in a new suit should be chosen only when a limit bid is inappropriate for one reason or another — usually because further exploration is needed to determine the best contract.

Choice of Suit

For the responder, the choice of suit can be boiled down to three simple rules.

1 With suits of unequal length, bid the longest.
2 With two five-card or longer suits, bid the higher-ranking.
3 With nothing but four-card suits, make the cheapest bid.

An obvious exception to the first rule occurs when you lack the strength to respond at the two-level.

a) ♠ : Q J 7 3   b) ♠ : Q J 7 3
   ♡ : 5 2   ♡ : 5 2
   ◇ : K 10 6 4 3   ◇ : A K J 4 3
   ♣ : 8 7   ♣ : 8 7

On hand (a) you should bid one diamond in response to an opening bid of one club, but respond one spade if partner opens one heart. You are not strong enough for a response of two diamonds, which would promise at least 8 points.

With hand (b) respond one diamond over one club and two diamonds over one heart. The hand is strong enough for two bids, and you can show the shorter spade suit on the second round.

c) ♠ : Q 9 8 4 3   d) ♠ : 7
   ♡ : 8 3   ♡ : K J 9 6 4
   ◇ : 7   ◇ : 10 5
   ♣ : A K 9 4 2   ♣ : A Q 10 8 5

With hand (c) respond one spade, the higher-ranking of your five-card suits, to an opening bid of one diamond or one heart. With (d) bid one heart in response to one diamond, and two hearts in response to one spade.

e) ♠ : A Q 8 5   f) ♠ : 6
   ♡ : J 10 9 5   ♡ : A Q 7 4
   ◇ : 8 5 3   ◇ : A K 6 2
   ♣ : 7 2   ♣ : Q J 7 3

On (e) bid one heart in response to an opening bid of one club or one diamond. Partner may be able to raise hearts or bid spades himself. In either case you will locate the 4–4 major trump fit if one exists. To respond one spade could result in 'losing' the heart suit.

Hand (f) is much stronger, but over an opening bid of one spade you should still make the cheapest suit bid available — in this case two clubs. By responding economically you leave space for partner to introduce a new suit at the two-level and retain every chance of locating the best contract.

Jumping for Joy

When you have upwards of 16 points and hear partner open the bidding, you can signal your elation, not by jumping up and down in your chair but by making a jump response in a new suit. This is a bid of one more than is necessary — two hearts in response to one club, for instance, or three diamonds in response to one spade. The jump shift, as it is sometimes called, indicates values in excess of those required for game and is therefore 'forcing to game'. Neither partner may pass until a game contract has been reached.

a) ♠: A K 6   b) ♠: 8 5
   ♡: 3   ♡: A K J 3
   ◇: A Q J 8 7   ◇: K 9 4
   ♣: A 7 4 2   ♣: A Q 10 3

On (a) jump to two diamonds in response to one club, to three diamonds in response to one heart or one spade, and to three clubs in response to one diamond. On (b) your response is two hearts over one club or one diamond, three clubs over one heart or one spade.

The requirements for the jump shift may be lowered when you have either a solid suit of your own or excellent support for partner.

c) ♠: A K Q J 9 3   d) ♠: 7
   ♡: 5 2   ♡: K J 9 5
   ◇: A J 3   ◇: A 6 3
   ♣: 8 4   ♣: A K 8 5 4

With (c) it is in order to force with two spades in response to one club, one diamond or one heart. Thereafter you can keep on bidding spades until partner wearies of the unequal struggle.

On (d) two clubs is enough in response to one diamond or one spade, but if partner opens one heart you can force with three clubs. Your intention is to support hearts on the next round, giving partner the picture of a hand too strong to raise immediately to four hearts.

Responding to 1 NT

The opening bid of one no trump, like all limit bids, is highly descriptive. You know that partner has from 15 to 17 points with a balanced distribution, and choosing the best contract is often just a matter of simple arithmetic. Bearing in mind that a combined total of 25 points will normally give a play for game, you should raise to three no trumps if you have 10 points and a fairly balanced hand.

a) ♠: Q J 4   b) ♠: 7 3
   ♡: 9 7   ♡: Q 8 5
   ◇: K 8 6 5   ◇: A K 9 6 5 4
   ♣: A 10 4 3   ♣: 10 3

Raise one no trump to three no trumps in both cases. Hand (b) is a point short, but there is ample compensation in the diamond length. On this type of hand there is no point in mentioning the diamond suit. Nine tricks in no trumps are likely to be easier to make than eleven in diamonds.

With 9 points (or a good 8 with a five-card suit) you should raise to two no trumps, inviting partner to continue to game if he has more than the minimum of 15 points.

All weaker balanced hands should be passed, since the prospects for game are negligible.

c) ♠: 10 8 3   d) ♠: 7 5 4
   ♡: K 9 5   ♡: A Q 3
   ◇: 7 6   ◇: Q 7 6 2
   ♣: K Q 10 6 4   ♣: 8 6 5

There are only 8 points on hand (c), but the useful intermediate cards (tens and nines) and the five-card club suit make it worth a raise to two no trumps. Hand (d) contains a barren 8 points and no distributional assets. You should pass.

Suit Responses

No trumps may not be the best spot when the responder has a distributional hand. A six-card or longer major suit provides a good alternative. When you have the values for game, bid it without further ado.

a) ♠: Q J 9 6 5 3   b) ♠: 8 4
   ♡: 2   ♡: K Q 8 5 4 2
   ◇: A K 5   ◇: A 7 6 5 3
   ♣: 8 6 3   ♣: —

Your response to one no trump should be four spades on (a) and four hearts on (b).

With a five-card major and game values, you can invite partner's help in deciding the best contract by jumping to three in your suit. This response is forcing to game.

c) ♠: K J 8 7 3   d) ♠: 7
   ♡: Q 10 5   ♡: J 10 9 5 2
   ◇: A 8 4   ◇: K Q 6
   ♣: 6 2   ♣: A J 8 3

Respond three spades on (c) and three hearts on (d). Partner will raise your suit with three-card or better support, but will revert to no trumps if he has a doubleton in your suit.

On weak distributional hands, bid your long suit at the two-level. The suit is likely to prove a better resting place than no trumps.

e) ♠: 5   f) ♠: 9 6 2
   ♡: J 9 7 6 5 3   ♡: 3
   ◇: 10 7 5 4   ◇: K Q 7 5 2
   ♣: 8 2   ♣: J 9 6 4

Respond two hearts on (e) and two diamonds on (f). In response to one no trump the bid of two in a suit is a cry of weakness. Opener should not bid again.

TIP FOR TODAY
*When you know the right contract, go
straight there. The best bidding is
simple bidding.*

4. Rebids by Opener

Some of the best auctions are concluded on the first round of bidding. But on many hands it takes a second, and perhaps a third, round of bidding to clarify the picture and identify the target, whether it be a part-score, a game or a slam.

An opening bid of one in a suit may be made with anything from 11 to 20 points, but more precision is needed on the second round. For the purpose of rebidding it is convenient to classify opening bids as follows.

Minimum	—	14 points or fewer
Fair	—	15–16
Good	—	17–18
Maximum	—	19–20

Whenever possible, the opener should choose a rebid that reflects both his strength and his distribution. His task is easiest when the responder has made a limit bid, and we shall consider these situations first.

After a Response of 1 NT

The responder promises a balanced hand with from 6 to 9 points, and there can be little prospect of game if you have a minimum or even a fair hand. Pass if your hand is reasonably balanced, but bid again if your shape is unsuited to play at no trumps.

For example, after 1♡ — 1 NT:

a) ♠: Q 7   b) ♠: Q 8 3   c) ♠: 8
   ♡: K Q 9 8 5   ♡: A J 10 7 6 4   ♡: A Q 8 6 2
   ◇: 10 3   ◇: K J 6   ◇: K Q 9 4
   ♣: A K 6 2   ♣: 4   ♣: A 7 4

Pass   Bid 2♡   Bid 2◇

You pass on hand (a) because one no trump is likely to be as good a contract as any. Hand (b) is sure to play better in hearts, so you repeat your long suit. This is a weak, 'sign-off' bid and partner will pass. The singleton spade in (c) makes a no trump contract unattractive, and you offer partner a choice by bidding two diamonds. This is still a weak bid and partner will not be tempted to go higher. He will either pass or return to two hearts.

Game becomes a possibility when you have a good hand. You should then choose an encouraging rebid, either a raise in no trumps, a jump in your first suit or a jump in a new suit. After 1♠ — 1 NT:

d) ♠: A Q J 7 4   e) ♠: K Q 7 6 5 3   f) ♠: A J 8 5 3
   ♡: K 10 4   ♡: 6   ♡: A K 9 5
   ◇: A 10 7   ◇: A K 6   ◇: 2
   ♣: K 5   ♣: K Q 3   ♣: A Q 5

Raise to 2 NT   Jump to 3♠   Jump to 3♡

On hand (d) you expect partner to pass with 6 or 7 points but to continue to game with 8 or 9. On (e) the spade suit offers the best chance of game, and your jump rebid asks if partner can help in trumps. If so he bids game, if not he passes. On (f) your jump in a new suit forces partner to speak again. He may raise the hearts if he has four-card support. Otherwise he will return to spades or no trumps.

When you have a maximum opening bid you will want to be in game as soon as you hear your partner's response. Bid game directly either in no trumps or in your suit, or jump in a new suit to force another bid from partner.

After 1♡ — 1 NT:

g) ♠: J 7 4   h) ♠: 2   i) ♠: A K
   ♡: A K Q 10 5   ♡: K Q J 8 7 3   ♡: K Q 9 5 3
   ◇: A Q   ◇: A Q 5   ◇: A K 7 6 5
   ♣: K 8 3   ♣: A Q 6   ♣: 7

Raise to 3 NT   Jump to 4♡   Jump to 3◇

Your combined count on hand (g) is at least 25 points and you have a good five-card suit — enough to ensure a play for game at no trumps.

Hand (h) counts only to 18 points, but the good heart suit makes it worth a game call. On (i) you will proceed to game in either hearts or diamonds, depending on partner's next call.

After a Response of 2 NT

Even a minimum opening bid may offer prospects of game when partner indicates a balanced 11–12 count by responding two no trumps.
With a very weak hand, however, you may pass, or sign-off by repeating your long suit at minimum level. After 1 ♠ — 2 NT:

a) ♠: K J 9 4 3   b) ♠: K J 10 7 6 3
   ♡: A Q 3   ♡: A 7
   ◇: 8 6   ◇: Q J 3
   ♣: Q 6 2   ♣: 9 5

Pass on (a), and sign off with 3 ♠ on (b). Partner should pass when you bid 3 ♠.

With anything in the way of extra values, you can raise to three no trumps, jump to game in a long major, or bid a new suit at the three-level. After 1 ♡ — 2 NT:

c) ♠: J 5   d) ♠: 6   e) ♠: Q 9 5
   ♡: Q 10 8 7 3   ♡: Q J 9 8 5 4   ♡: A K 10 6 2
   ◇: A Q 9   ◇: K 10 2   ◇: 4
   ♣: A J 5   ♣: A K 7   ♣: K Q 10 8

   Raise to 3 NT   Bid 4 ♡   Bid 3 ♣

The bid of a new suit, as in example (e), is forcing, but the responder should be wary of raising the second suit if it is a minor. He is really being asked to choose between your major suit and no trumps.

After a Response of 3 NT

Opener should usually pass, but may rebid a long major suit, or bid a new suit if he has a two-suited hand. With a good or maximum opening he may consider a slam try (see Chapter 7).

After a Single Raise

When partner gives a single raise in your suit, pass with a minimum opening, but consider trying for game with a fair or good hand. There is some overlapping in our classification of opening bids. A fair hand in high cards may become good when a trump fit is found. A long suit becomes particularly valuable when partner supports it. Go straight to game in your major suit when you can count seven probable winners in your own hand.

A rebid of three in a new suit is termed a trial bid. It asks partner to bid game if he has a good raise with some help in the 'trial' suit. Otherwise he can sign off by bidding three in your suit.

A rebid of two no trumps indicates a balanced hand of 17–18 points. Partner can then judge whether to pass, sign off in three of your suit, raise to three no trumps, or jump to four of your suit.

With a maximum opening you should bid game either in your suit or, if your pattern is suitable, in no trumps.

After 1 ♡ — 2 ♡:

a)	b)	c)
♠: K J 8	♠: A K 6	♠: K 8 3
♡: A K 10 6 2	♡: K Q 8 7 5	♡: K J 9 5
◇: K 4 3	◇: 3	◇: A J 7 5
♣: 8 7	♣: K 10 7 3	♣: A Q
Pass	Bid 3 ♣	Bid 2 NT

After your trial bid of three clubs on hand (b), partner should consider both his general strength and his club holding in deciding whether to bid three hearts or four. A doubleton ace or doubleton queen would be a favourable club holding. So would a singleton or a void if he has plenty of trumps. Three small clubs would be a poor holding.

After the same sequence of 1 ♡ — 2 ♡:

d)	e)	f)
♠: Q 6	♠: A Q 8	♠: Q J 2
♡: A K 10 7 6	♡: Q 9 8 6 4 3	♡: A J 10 8
◇: K 3	◇: A Q J 5	◇: A K 9
♣: A K 5 3	♣: —	♣: K J 7
Bid 4 ♡	Bid 4 ♡	Bid 3 NT

No need for a trial bid on hand (d). With a maximum opening bid just go straight to game. On (e) you have only 15 points, but when partner supports hearts it becomes a very powerful hand, well worth a game bid. On (f) you have a balanced maximum and your rebid is three no trumps. Partner will return to hearts if he has four or more trumps.

After a Double Raise

When partner raises your major suit to three, accept the invitation to bid game unless your hand is an absolute minimum and short of aces. For example, after 1 ♡ — 3 ♡:

a)	b)
♠: 7	♠: 7
♡: K Q 8 7 3	♡: A J 7 6 3
◇: K J 7 5	◇: A 9 8 4
♣: Q J 2	♣: K 6 4

Pass on hand (a) but bid four hearts on (b).

When your minor suit is raised to three, consider the possibility of playing in no trumps. In general you should pass with a minimum hand but bid again with anything better. After 1 ◇ — 3 ◇ :

c) ♠: Q 7
   ♡: K J 3
   ◇: A Q 10 4
   ♣: J 9 4 3

   Pass

d) ♠: A 6
   ♡: K 9
   ◇: A J 9 6 5 3
   ♣: Q 10 8

   Bid 3 NT

e) ♠: 5
   ♡: K Q 10 9
   ◇: A K J 8 3
   ♣: Q 8 6

   Bid 3 ♡

On hand (e) your bid of three hearts is, of course, forcing. You hope that partner will now be able to bid three no trumps.

After a Raise to Game

When partner raises your opening major suit bid to four, it is normally right to pass. With a good or maximum hand, however, you may consider making a slam try (see Chapter 7).

After a Response in a New Suit

The response in a new suit is unlimited and forcing, and you must therefore find another bid. Partner may be quite strong, but when he responds at the one-level he may have as few as 6 points, so you must be cautious when you are weak. Let us consider the rebids that are available for the different categories of opening bids.

1 *Minimum Hands.* Here the choice lies between a rebid of 1 NT, a repeat of your first suit, a single raise of partner's suit, and the bid of a new suit at the one-level (or at the two-level if the new suit is lower ranking than your first suit).

The rebid of 1 NT shows a balanced hand of 13–14 points — a hand too weak for an opening bid of 1 NT. After 1 ♣ — 1 ♡ :

a) ♠: J 9 7 3
   ♡: A J 5
   ◇: Q J 5
   ♣: A 10 3

   Rebid 1 NT

b) ♠: K Q 6
   ♡: Q 2
   ◇: A 8 5
   ♣: K 9 8 4 2

   Rebid 1 NT

A rebid of your original suit indicates a minimum hand with a six-card or a good five-card suit. After 1 ♡ — 1 ♠ :

c) ♠: Q 5
   ♡: K 10 9 6 5 2
   ◇: 9 4 3
   ♣: A K

   Rebid 2 ♡

d) ♠: A 7
   ♡: A Q J 9 4
   ◇: Q 7 6
   ♣: 8 3 2

   Rebid 2 ♡

A single raise of partner's suit shows a minimum hand with three-card or better trump support. After 1 ◇ — 1 ♠:

e) ♠: Q 10 3　　f) ♠: J 6 5 2
　♡: 7 4　　　　♡: 4
　◇: A K 10 5 2　◇: A Q 8 7 5
　♣: A 7 5　　　♣: K Q 6

　Raise to 2 ♠　　Raise to 2 ♠

On these hands a raise of partner's major suit is preferable to a rebid of your own minor.

When partner responds two hearts to your opening bid of one spade, it is reasonable to raise him on a minimum hand with heart support. You can always count on partner for at least five hearts on this sequence. With no more than four hearts he would either respond in no trumps or bid a lower ranking suit first.

g) ♠: A J 9 8 3
　♡: Q J 7
　◇: 4
　♣: A 9 6 3

Raise partner's response of two hearts to three hearts.

However, try to avoid raising partner's minor suit response to the three-level on a minimum hand. You should ideally have better values for this raise, but you may occasionally have to stretch a point.

h) ♠: A J 7 6
　♡: 7 2
　◇: K Q 4 2
　♣: A 10 5

You open one diamond on this hand, intending to rebid one spade over a response of one heart. If instead partner makes the awkward response of two clubs, there is no sensible alternative to a raise to three clubs.

The rebid of any new suit at the one-level, or a lower-ranking suit at the two-level, promises no more than a minimum hand. This is an un-limited rebid, however, and may also be made on quite strong hands. After 1 ◇ — 1 ♡:

i) ♠: K Q 9 4　j) ♠: 8 5
　♡: 3　　　　　♡: Q 2
　◇: A 9 8 5 3　◇: K J 10 4 2
　♣: K J 5　　　♣: A K 8 7

　Rebid 1 ♠　　　Rebid 2 ♣

2 *Fair Hands*. Since you rebid 1 NT to show 13–14, you must not make the same bid with a better hand. In any case, with a balanced hand of 15–16 points you will normally open 1 NT. Occasionally you may prefer to open one in a suit because of some slight imbalance in the hand. If partner then responds at the two-level in your weak spot, you can indicate your values with a rebid of 2 NT.

For example, after 1 ♠ — 2 ♡:

a) ♠: A K Q 10 3   b) ♠: A Q J 4 2
   ♡: 4 3   ♡: J 5
   ◇: K 8 2   ◇: Q 9 6 2
   ♣: Q J 6   ♣: A Q

   Rebid 2 NT   Rebid 2 NT

Responder should raise to 3 NT with 10 points.

With a fair hand you may give either a single or a double raise in partner's major suit, depending on your trump support and distribution. A single raise will generally be right with three trumps, a double raise with four trumps and a singleton or void. After 1 ◇ — 1 ♡:

c) ♠: 7   d) ♠: 5
   ♡: Q 9 3   ♡: K 10 4 3
   ◇: A K 7 6 2   ◇: A K 7 5 4
   ♣: A Q 8 5   ♣: A Q 5

   Raise to 2 ♡   Raise to 3 ♡

You need have no inhibitions about raising a minor suit to the three-level when you have 15–16 points. After 1 ♡ — 2 ♣:

e) ♠: 6   f) ♠: 10 8 7 3
   ♡: A K 6 5   ♡: A Q J 8 6
   ◇: A Q J 8   ◇: 2
   ♣: J 10 7 2   ♣: A K Q

   Raise to 3 ♣   Raise to 3 ♣

Avoid making a minimum rebid in your original suit when you have a fair hand, but consider a jump rebid if you have a good six-card major suit. After 1 ♡ — 2 ♣:

g) ♠: A Q 5   h) ♠: 8 5
   ♡: K Q J 9 7 3   ♡: A Q 10 9 6 3
   ◇: 4   ◇: A K J
   ♣: K 7 6   ♣: Q 7

   Rebid 3 ♡   Rebid 3 ♡

These jump rebids are not forcing but are highly encouraging. Responder may pass with a minimum hand but should continue to game with any extra values.

With a fair hand you can still bid a new suit at the one-level, and at the two-level you need not restrict yourself to bidding a lower-ranking suit. You may show your full values by rebidding in a higher-ranking suit. After 1 ♣ — 1 ♡:

i) ♠: K J 7 5   j) ♠: 7 4
   ♡: 2   ♡: K 6
   ◇: A Q 7   ◇: A K 7 5
   ♣: A Q 8 7 3   ♣: K Q J 6 4

   Rebid 1 ♠   Rebid 2 ◇

In the absence of a trump fit, you have to make do with a rebid of one spade on hand (i). This is the same rebid that you would have made on a minimum hand. On (j) you can give better indication of your strength by rebidding two diamonds. Your partner is compelled to go to the three-level if he prefers clubs, but your hand is strong enough to stand it. This sequence of bids — an opening bid in a suit followed by a rebid in a higher-ranking suit at the two-level — is known as a 'reverse'. It guarantees at least 15 points.

On a fair hand with good distribution it is also in order to introduce a new suit at the three-level. This 'high reverse', as it is called, is forcing for one round and promises a further bid. After 1 ♠ — 2 ◇:

k) ♠: K Q 10 6 5 3
   ♡: —
   ◇: Q 6
   ♣: A K J 8 4

   Rebid 3 ♣

3 *Good Hands.* When your opening bid is in the 17–18 point range, you should normally jump to show your strength on the second round. The choices are a jump in no trumps, a double or treble raise in partner's suit, a jump in your own suit, and the unlimited rebid in a new suit.

A jump in no trumps is the right action on balanced hands. After a response of one in a suit your rebid is two no trumps. After a response of two in a suit it is three no trumps.

After 1 ♡ — 1 ♠:   After 1 ♡ — 2 ♣:

a) ♠: Q 5   b) ♠: A Q 5
   ♡: A K J 9 6   ♡: K Q 7 4
   ◇: K 10 3   ◇: A Q 10 7
   ♣: A 9 8   ♣: J 8

   Rebid 2 NT   Rebid 3 NT

A double raise in partner's major suit promises four-card trump support. With particularly good distribution and four trumps, raise all the way to game. After 1 ◇ — 1 ♠:

c) ♠: Q 8 7 2   d) ♠: Q J 8 4
   ♡: A K   ♡: 3
   ◇: K 10 8 5 4   ◇: A K Q 5 2
   ♣: K Q   ♣: K Q 6

   Raise to 3 ♠   Raise to 4 ♠

The jump rebid in your own suit shows, as always, a powerful hand that needs a little help from partner to make game. Don't jump to three when you are good enough for four. After 1 ♡ — 1 ♠:

e) ♠: 2   f) ♠: Q 6 4
   ♡: A K J 10 6 5   ♡: A K J 10 6 5
   ◇: Q 6 4   ◇: 2
   ♣: A K 3   ♣: A K 3

   Rebid 3 ♡   Rebid 4 ♡

The difference between the two hands lies in the spade fit. Three cards headed by the queen in the suit bid by partner are likely to be more useful than the same holding in a side suit.

Even with a good hand you will sometimes have to settle for a simple change of suit. After 1 ♣ — 1 ◇:

g) ♠: A K Q 3
   ♡: 6 3
   ◇: K 5
   ♣: A J 9 7 6

   Rebid 1 ♠

You have a good hand, but game must be unlikely if partner cannot squeeze out another bid.

4 *Maximum Hands.* When you have a maximum opening bid and partner finds a response, it is up to you to make sure that the bidding does not die below game. Three no trumps is your rebid on balanced hands of 19–20 points. If your distribution is unbalanced, you must force to game by making a jump rebid in a new suit.

After 1 ◇ — 1 ♡:

a) ♠: K Q 10   b) ♠: 5
   ♡: 9 4   ♡: A K 6
   ◇: A Q 8 6 5   ◇: K Q J 4 3
   ♣: A K J   ♣: A Q J 4

   Rebid 3 NT   Rebid 3 ♣

On hand (b) the values for game are present, but at this stage you cannot be sure of the best contract. You therefore create a game-forcing situation by jumping to three clubs. This allows for a leisurely investigation of the optimum game contract.

After a Force by Responder

When the response to your opening bid is a jump shift, you must keep the bidding open until game is reached. In general you should make your natural rebid, of necessity one level higher than it would otherwise have been.

After 1 ♠ — 3 ◇, for instance:

a) ♠: A Q 9 8 6 3
   ♡: K 7 5
   ◇: K 4
   ♣: 8 4

   Rebid 3 ♠

b) ♠: A J 10 6 3
   ♡: K 9 7 4 3
   ◇: 7
   ♣: A 2

   Rebid 3 ♡

c) ♠: K Q 7 6 5
   ♡: 2
   ◇: K J 4 2
   ♣: A Q 3

   Rebid 4 ◇

d) ♠: A Q 10 5 2
   ♡: K 9 6
   ◇: J 7
   ♣: A J 5

   Rebid 3 NT

TIP FOR TODAY

*Try to make life easy for partner
by limiting your hand at the
earliest opportunity.*

5. Rebids by Responder

The longer the auction goes on, the greater the risk of complication. The reason is not hard to see. When an opening bid in any one of four suits is permutated with a number of responses and an even greater number of rebids, the possibilities begin to multiply like rabbits. Fortunately there is no need to deal separately with each situation that the responder may be called upon to face on the second round of bidding. A little general advice will cover all the common cases.

When Opener Rebids in a New Suit

We have seen that a simple change of suit by the opener may be made on a minimum hand and also on quite a good hand. The rebid is not strictly limited, but neither is it forcing. Responder may pass if he has a weak hand and prefers the second suit.

Those last few words contain the key to the correct action in this situation. Holding a weak hand, the responder is expected to 'give preference', to indicate which of opener's suits he prefers. Bearing in mind that the opener bids his longest suit first, the responder should pass only if he has more cards in the second suit. He should return to the first suit if he has an equal number of cards in each. This shows no more strength than a pass. It is simply a conversion to what is likely to be the better trump suit.

After an opening bid of one heart, a response of one spade and a rebid of two diamonds, for instance:

a) ♠: K J 9 4 3 b) ♠: K J 9 4 3
   ♡: 9 5   ♡: K 6
   ◇: K 6   ◇: 9 8 5
   ♣: 8 7 5 3   ♣: 7 5 3

   Rebid 2 ♡   Pass

Avoid taking the same weak action on stronger hands. With fair values in support of either of partner's suits go to the three-level.

Assuming the same start to the auction, 1 ♡ — 1 ♠ — 2 ◇:

c) ♠: A 9 8 5 2 d) ♠: A 9 8 5 2
   ♡: Q J 4   ♡: Q 4
   ◇: K 4   ◇: K J 6 4
   ♣: 7 6 5   ♣: 7 5

   Jump to 3 ♡   Raise to 3 ◇

The above hands contain useful cards in both of partner's suits as well as an outside ace. On (c) you give jump preference to three hearts, and on (d) you raise the diamonds.

You may, of course, have no liking for either of partner's suits. There is no law against bidding no trumps with suitable values (11–12 points) or rebidding a good suit of your own. A new suit bid at the three-level shows a strong hand and is forcing to game. After 1 ♡ — 1 ♠ — 2 ◇:

e) ♠: K J 7 4 3   f) ♠: K J 10 8 7 3   g) ♠: A Q J 7 4
   ♡: 8 7   ♡: 7 5   ♡: 4
   ◇: Q 5   ◇: 9 2   ◇: Q 2
   ♣: A J 9 2   ♣: A 8 5   ♣: K Q 9 6 2

   Rebid 2 NT   Rebid 2 ♠   Rebid 3 ♣

After a Minimum Rebid

When opener makes a minimum rebid either in his suit, in your suit or in no trumps, it is wise to abandon hope of game if you have 10 points or fewer. With 11 points you should generally make a further effort. After 1 ♡ — 1 ♠ — 2 ♡:

a) ♠: K Q 9 4   b) ♠: K Q 6 4 2   c) ♠: A J 8 6
   ♡: 8 3   ♡: Q 7 2   ♡: J 8
   ◇: J 7 6   ◇: A 8 7   ◇: Q 10 5 4
   ♣: K 7 3 2   ♣: 5 2   ♣: K 10 3

   Pass   Raise to 3 ♡   Bid 2 NT

Remember that some sort of fit with partner's suit is of critical importance. Demote your high cards when you are short in partner's long suit. After 1 ♡ — 1 ♠ — 2 ♡:

d) ♠: A 10 8 3 2
   ♡: —
   ◇: K Q 7 2
   ♣: Q 9 6 5

A pass is indicated in spite of your 11 points, for the hand has all the hallmarks of a misfit. Pay no attention to that inner voice that asks whether you are a man or a mouse. Squeak out a pass and you will live to fight another day.

Conversely, let boldness be your friend when the hands appear to fit well. After 1 ♡ — 1 ♠ — 2 ♠:

e) ♠: K Q 9 5   f) ♠: Q 10 8 5 4   g) ♠: Q J 8 5
   ♡: 8 6   ♡: K 9 3   ♡: K 6
   ◇: A 5 4 2   ◇: 7 4   ◇: A 7 4
   ♣: 9 7 3   ♣: A 8 7   ♣: J 10 3 2

   Pass   Bid 3 ♠   Bid 2 NT

On hand (f) there appears to be a good fit in two suits, so you can write up your 9 points and try for game in spades.

After 1 ♡ — 1 ♠ — 1 NT:

h) ♠: A J 8 4   i) ♠: A 10 9 7 6 3   j) ♠: A 10 9 5 4
   ♡: 7 2   ♡: 6   ♡: J 10 6
   ◇: K Q 5   ◇: Q 8 3   ◇: 6 5 .
   ♣: 8 5 4 3   ♣: 8 7 5   ♣: A K 7

   Pass   Bid 2 ♠   Bid 3 ♡

On hand (h) your maximum combined count is 24. This is not enough for game and there is no point in bidding again. Hand (i) is sure to play better in spades than no trumps. When you sign off in two spades partner should pass. On hand (j) you have the values for a raise to three no trumps, but the best contract may be four of a major suit. The forcing jump to three hearts keeps all your options open. If partner has five hearts he will bid game in that suit. Alternatively, partner may have three spades, and when he shows this support you can go on to four spades. Lacking five hearts or three spades, partner will revert to three no trumps.

TIP FOR TODAY

Remember that a great deal
depends on the fit.

6. Strong Opening Bids

They say that it is better to be lucky than good. I am not in a position to comment on your virtue, but I can guarantee that you will sometimes be lucky enough to hold a hand that is too strong for an opening bid of one in a suit, a hand that will produce game even if partner contributes nothing but a shapeless collection of tram-tickets.

♠: A K Q 10 4
♡: A K 10 8 3
◇: A 3
♣: 6

If you hold this hand, for example, you can be fairly confident of making game in one of the major suits. You cannot take the risk of opening one spade, for if partner has a weak hand he will pass and game will be missed. Yet you can hardly open four spades, for that may not be the right contract.

On this sort of hand you need to buy a little time to investigate the best contract, and you do this by making a conventional opening bid of two clubs.

Opening 2 ♣

A conventional bid is one that has a meaning quite different from its natural meaning. It is an artificial bid, in fact. The opening bid of two clubs does not promise a club suit. It is merely a convenient way of indicating game-going values. The message to partner is as follows: 'I have a whale of a hand, which I shall describe in the next couple of rounds of bidding. Keep the bidding open until game is reached, no matter how weak your hand.'

The opener thereafter bids his hand naturally, secure in the knowledge that his partner will not pass.

Negative Response

With a weak hand containing less than 7 points, the responder gives the negative response of two diamonds. Again this is a purely conventional bid, bearing no relationship to the diamond holding.

Let us place a yarborough (a hand containing no honour card) opposite our big hand and see how the bidding should develop.

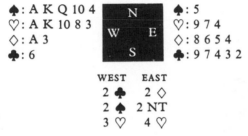

♠ : A K Q 10 4		♠ : 5
♡ : A K 10 8 3		♡ : 9 7 4
♢ : A 3		♢ : 8 6 5 4
♣ : 6		♣ : 9 7 4 3 2

WEST	EAST
2 ♣	2 ♢
2 ♠	2 NT
3 ♡	4 ♡

After the forcing opening bid of two clubs and the negative response of two diamonds, West bids the higher-ranking of his suits. With no spade support and no good suit of his own, East keeps the ball rolling by bidding two no trumps. West then introduces his second suit and East reluctantly raises to game.

Four hearts is a reasonable contract on these hands. After winning the ace of spades the declarer can trump his small spade with one of dummy's hearts. If the suits break normally he will make ten tricks, losing only one heart, one diamond and one club.

Having given a negative response of two diamonds, the responder need not be reluctant to show a five-card suit on the next round of bidding. Consider this example.

♠: A Q 8 7 4 3   ♠: 2
♡: A K 6   ♡: Q J 7 5 2
◇: A K Q   ◇: 9 5 4
♣: 3   ♣: 10 8 4 2

WEST   EAST
2 ♣   2 ◇
2 ♠   3 ♡
4 ♡   No bid

Having denied positive values with his first response, East feels free to introduce his heart suit on the next round. Four hearts is by far the best game contract, but it cannot be reached unless East bids the suit.

Positive Responses

When partner opens two clubs, give a positive response when you have 7 or more points including at least one ace or two kings.

a) ♠: K 7 6   b) ♠: A Q J 9 3   c) ♠: Q 7 5
   ♡: 10 5 2   ♡: 8 7 3   ♡: 5 4
   ◇: K 9 6 3   ◇: 4 2   ◇: A K 10 4 2
   ♣: Q 5 4   ♣: 7 4 3   ♣: 8 3 2

   Respond 2 NT   Respond 2 ♠   Respond 3 ◇

Note that, since two diamonds is the negative, you have to jump to give a positive response in diamonds.

Requirements for 2 ♣

We need to define more closely the requirements for an opening bid of two clubs. The big hands fall into two categories.

1 Distributional hands with upwards of 20 points and an expectancy of taking at least nine tricks.

2 Balanced hands containing at least 23 points.

After opening two clubs on a balanced hand, you rebid two no trumps with 23–24 points, three no trumps with 25–27.

An Exception

The opening bid of two clubs is forcing to game — except when the opener rebids two no trumps after a negative response. A balanced hand of 23 or 24 points needs a little help to make game, and responder is permitted to pass when he has a worthless hand. With as much as a queen and a jack, however, responder should bid three no trumps or make a forcing response of three in a suit.

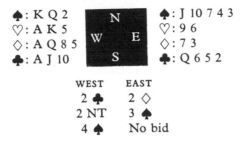

♠: K Q 2
♡: A K 5
◇: A Q 8 5
♣: A J 10

♠: J 10 7 4 3
♡: 9 6
◇: 7 3
♣: Q 6 5 2

WEST	EAST
2 ♣	2 ◇
2 NT	3 ♠
4 ♠	No bid

With just enough strength to move over two no trumps, East bids his major suit and is raised to game. Four spades would be unlucky to fail on this hand, whereas three no trumps would be lucky to succeed.

Opening Two Bids in Other Suits

Hands that are almost, but not quite, good enough to force to game may be opened with bids of two spades, two hearts or two diamonds. These bids promise at least eight tricks in the opening hand and are forcing for one round only. Responder may pass on the second round if he has nothing to contribute.

The opener's hand may be either single-suited or two-suited and the normal point range is from 14 to 19.

a) ♠: A K Q J 9 8 3
   ♡: 7
   ◇: A 10 8
   ♣: 9 2

Open 2 ♠

b) ♠: 4
   ♡: K Q 9 8 6 2
   ◇: A
   ♣: A Q J 10 5

Open 2 ♡

c) ♠: A Q
   ♡: K J 10
   ◇: A K J 10 8 7 5
   ♣: 2

Open 2 ◇

Negative Response

This time the negative response is two no trumps, and it may be given on quite a fair hand when there is no constructive alternative. When partner opens two hearts:

a) ♠: 9 7 4
   ♡: 6 3 2
   ◇: J 9 7 4
   ♣: 8 7 2

Respond 2 NT

b) ♠: Q J 5
   ♡: 6 3
   ◇: K 10 4 2
   ♣: Q 8 7 2

Respond 2 NT

c) ♠: K J 5
   ♡: Q 6
   ◇: Q 9 7 4
   ♣: K 10 4 3

Respond 3 NT

On hand (a) you will naturally pass on the next round, unless partner forces you to bid again by jumping in a new suit. On (b) you will continue to game after partner's rebid. The response on (c) is three no trumps, indicating the sort of hand on which you would respond two no trumps to an opening bid of one heart.

Positive Responses

A single raise may be given on any hand that contains trump support and an ace. A double raise is reserved for hands with good trump support but no ace or void. When partner opens two hearts:

a) ♠: 8 4
♡: Q 7 5
◇: 10 8 7 4 2
♣: A 9 5

Raise to 3 ♡

b) ♠: K 7 6 2
♡: K J 3
◇: 6 5
♣: 10 7 4 3

Raise to 4 ♡

A response in a new suit may be made when you have a good five-card or longer suit and upwards of 7 points. A little extra strength is advisable if you have to go to the three-level.

When opener bids two hearts:

c) ♠: K Q 10 7 4
♡: 5 2
◇: K 8 5 3
♣: 9 7

Respond 2 ♠

d) ♠: 9 4 3
♡: 2
◇: A K J 8 5
♣: Q 8 7 2

Respond 3 ◇

Opening 2 NT

The only type of strong hand that we have not so far considered is the balanced hand of 20–22 points with a stopper in every suit. This hand is shown by an opening bid of two no trumps.

a) ♠: Q J 4
♡: A J 9
◇: K 7
♣: A K Q 8 3

Open 2 NT

b) ♠: A K 6
♡: K Q 3 2
◇: K J 7 3
♣: A Q

Open 2 NT

This is a limit bid and therefore not forcing. Responder may pass if unable to help, but with about 5 points he should raise to three no trumps or bid a five-card major suit.

TIP FOR TODAY

When partner opens two in a suit, don't pass without first calling an ambulance.

7. Bidding a Slam

There is nothing in this game to equal the thrill of bidding and making your first slam. Large bonuses are awarded for successful slams (see the scoring table on page 96), making the venture profitable as well as supremely satisfying. A slam that fails represents a sure game lost, however, damaging both your pocket book and your morale.

The chance of a slam will come your way roughly once in every twenty deals, but you should not attempt them all. Contracting for twelve or thirteen tricks is a risky business, and I suggest that while you are finding your feet at bridge you should bid only those slams that appear sure to succeed. Don't worry if you find yourself making twelve tricks when you have bid no higher than game. It does not pay to be too ambitious.

The time to consider a slam is when you become aware of excess strength, over and above that needed for game, in the combined hands. A positive response to an opening bid of two clubs indicates that you are close to the slam zone. So does a jump shift by the responder when the opener has a fair hand, or a jump rebid by the opener when the responder has opening values.

The point count is a reliable guide on balanced hands, where a combined total of 34 points will normally produce a small slam. A least there is no danger of the defenders cashing the first two tricks. The most they can have is 6 points — an ace and a queen, perhaps, or two kings.

Direct Slam Bidding

Many slams are bid by an extension of normal game-bidding methods. If the early bidding is soundly based, it is just a matter of doing your sums correctly. Suppose that partner opens one club and rebids three no trumps over your response of one diamond.

♠ : J 5 3
♡ : A J 6 3
◇ : A Q 8 5
♣ : K 2

You have 15 points and partner has promised 19, bringing you up to the magic total of 34. There is no need to beat about the bush. Just raise to six no trumps. The only cause for regret is that partner will have the fun of playing it instead of you.

When you are uncertain if the required strength is present you can invite partner's co-operation by bidding beyond game without committing your side to slam. Suppose partner opens two no trumps.

♠: A J 6
♡: Q 7 4
◇: 9 6 2
♣: K Q 10 3

Your 12 points may not be enough for slam if partner has a minimum 20-count. Your bid is therefore four no trumps, a strong slam invitation. Partner is expected to pass with a minimum and bid six no trumps with a maximum. If he has an in-between count of 21, you will soon discover whether he is an optimist or a pessimist.

On distributional hands where there is a good trump fit, a small slam may be made with considerably less than 34 points. When the opponents have 8 or more points, however, there is always the danger that they may have two aces. It is depressing to bid a slam and then watch helplessly as the defenders take the first two tricks.

One way of avoiding this hazard is by the use of the Blackwood slam convention.

Blackwood

This is a conventional method of checking the number of aces held by the partnership. When a trump suit has been firmly agreed, a bid of four no trumps is artificial and asks partner how many aces he has.

The responses are as follows:

5 ♣   no ace or four
5 ◇   one ace
5 ♡   two aces
5 ♠   three aces

The cheapest response of five clubs normally shows no aces, but it may also show all four. There is not likely to be any confusion, for the previous bidding will indicate which alternative is possible.

Here is the sort of hand on which Blackwood can be helpful.

♠: K Q 10 7 6 3
♡: K Q
◇: 6
♣: A K Q 7

You open two spades and hear a response of three spades, which promises an ace. Partner may of course have more than one ace, in which case you can expect to make a slam. You therefore set the Blackwood wheels in motion with a bid of four no trumps. If you receive the disappointing response of five diamonds you will have to settle in five spades. But if partner shows two aces by bidding five hearts you will go on to six spades, and if his response is five spades you will bid a confident grand slam.

Blackwood is such a simple convention and such fun to use that you may be tempted to give it an airing on unsuitable occasions. Do not use it unless you are sure that the strength for a slam is present, and do not use it unless you have agreed a trump suit. Your only concern should be the number of aces in the combined hands. Blackwood is best regarded not as an aid to slam bidding but as a means of keeping out of slams that cannot be made.

Here is an example.

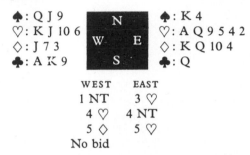

♠: Q J 9
♡: K J 10 6
◇: J 7 3
♣: A K 9

♠: K 4
♡: A Q 9 5 4 2
◇: K Q 10 4
♣: Q

WEST	EAST
1 NT	3 ♡
4 ♡	4 NT
5 ◇	5 ♡
No bid	

With plenty of surplus strength, East has high hopes, but he has to subside in five hearts when he learns that two aces are missing.

Note that the player who bids four no trumps assumes the captaincy of the partnership for the duration of the auction. It is up to him to determine the final contract, and his partner should respect his decision.

Be particularly wary of using Blackwood when your trump suit is a minor. If your suit is clubs, for instance, you cannot afford to bid four no trumps with only one ace in your own hand. If partner also has only one ace his response of five diamonds will carry you too high.

Checking on Kings

When the response to four no trumps confirms that all the aces are present, you may, if interested in a grand slam, continue with a bid of five no trumps to ask for kings. This is an extension of the Blackwood convention, and the responses are on a similar schedule.

6 ♣ no king
6 ◇ one king
6 ♡ two kings
6 ♠ three kings
6 NT all four kings

This enquiry for kings can be helpful on certain hands, but I suggest that you leave grand slams alone until you have confidence in your ability to handle lesser contracts.

Cue Bidding

An alternative method of checking up on aces is much favoured by experienced players. When the trump suit has been agreed, the bid of a new suit at a high level is termed a cue bid. It shows first-round control (either the ace or a void) in the suit. Instead of asking partner about his aces, you tell him about yours, at the same time inviting him to express an opinion about slam prospects. Partner opens one heart, for example, and raises your response of one spade to three spades.

♠ : A Q J 7 5
♡ : Q 6
◇ : 7 6 3
♣ : A 9 4

With this hand you know that you must be close to the slam zone, so you show your ace of clubs by bidding four clubs. What you would like to hear from partner is a return cue bid of four diamonds, which would encourage you to bid six spades. If instead partner bids four hearts, you must revert to four spades and leave further action to him.

Do not attempt to use cue bids at the moment, but bear in mind that you will probably find them useful one day.

TIP FOR TODAY

Never use Blackwood unless you
know where you are going.

8. Pre-emptive Bidding

So far in our study of bidding technique we have been concerned solely with reaching our best contract. That is the proper objective when our side has most of the high cards, but when the position is reversed our aim must be to prevent the opponents from making the best of their cards. One way of achieving this is by opening with a bid of three or four in a suit.

Such bids are not strong in high cards, but are based on long suits of seven or eight cards. They are known as pre-emptive or shut-out bids. The idea is to put up a barrage high enough to shut the opponents out of the auction, or at least to make it hard for them to reach their best contract.

Often the opponents will elect to double you rather than risk bidding at the four or five-level. It follows that you cannot afford to be too daring with your pre-emptive bids, or you may suffer an excessive penalty. To provide a reasonable margin of safety, you should be within three tricks of your contract in your own hand if you are not vulnerable, and within two tricks if vulnerable.

Here are some examples.

a) ♠: 7
   ♡: K Q J 10 8 6 3
   ◇: J 7 3
   ♣: 8 4

b) ♠: Q J 10 7 6 5 4 2
   ♡: 6
   ◇: K Q J
   ♣: 5

On hand (a) you expect to make six tricks with hearts as trumps. Open three hearts if not vulnerable, but pass if vulnerable. Hand (b) is worth eight tricks playing in spades. Open four spades whether vulnerable or not.

Note that these are hands that do not qualify for an opening bid of one in a suit because of the lack of high cards.

In a minor suit a pre-emptive bid may even be made at the five-level. Here is an example.

♠: —
♡: 9 2
◇: 6 4
♣: A K J 10 8 7 6 3 2

Open five clubs whether vulnerable or not. At least it will keep your partner from falling asleep.

Responding to Three-Bids

In his eagerness to shut out the opponents, partner may occasionally hit the wrong target, shutting you out instead. It will generally pay you to stay shut out. There is not much point in mentioning a suit of your own when partner is unlikely to be able to support it.

To raise an opening bid of three in a major to game, you need three supporting winners when vulnerable and four when not vulnerable. Trump support is not necessary since the suit should be self-supporting, but be conservative in counting your supporting tricks. Aces are what partner will most like to see in your hand. If partner opens three hearts, for example:

♠: A 9 5
♡: 6
◇: A K 4 2
♣: J 8 7 3 2

Raise to four hearts when you are vulnerable, but pass when not vulnerable. If partner opens three spades, you can hope to make an extra trick by trumping a heart in your hand and can therefore raise to four spades whether vulnerable or not.

A response of three no trumps guarantees good stoppers in the side suits along with high cards in partner's suit.

♠ : A Q 5
♡ : K 10 3
◇ : A J 10
♣ : Q 10 8 3

Bid three no trumps in response to an opening three-bid in any suit.

Pre-emptive Responses

An attempt to shut out the enemy may still be worth while after your partner has opened the bidding. If partner opens one club and the next player passes:

a) ♠ : K J 10 9 8 5 3   b) ♠ : 7
   ♡ : 2   ♡ : K Q 10 9 8 6 3 2
   ◇ : 8 7   ◇ : 9 5
   ♣ : J 10 2   ♣ : J 3

Respond 3 ♠   Respond 4 ♡

These responses show much the same sort of hand as an opening bid of three or four in a suit.

Note that a pre-emptive response is always a double or a triple jump in a new suit. Do not confuse these bids with the single jump in a new suit, which denotes a strong hand and is forcing to game.

Countering Pre-emptive Bids

Let us move around the table and see what a pre-emptive bid feels like from the receiving end. Your right-hand opponent opens three spades and you hold:

♠ : 6
♡ : K J 8 5
◇ : A K 7 3
♣ : A Q 9 5

Now you know. It feels distinctly unpleasant, and your first impulse may be to let your tormentor have the contents of the ashtray over the head. You need to take some action on this good hand, for a pass may lead to a missed game. Partner is likely to have a good fit in one of your suits, but it would be highly dangerous for you to indulge in a guessing game by bidding a suit at the four-level.

Various conventional methods have been designed to cope with this situation. Perhaps the simplest is to treat a bid of three no trumps as an artificial request for your partner to bid his best suit. You will not always land on your feet, but at least you will have a chance.

When you have a good hand with strength in the enemy suit you can double in the hope of exacting a penalty.

♠: A Q 9 5
♡: Q 7 2
◇: A K 7 3
♣: K 7

Double an opening bid of three spades on this hand.

TIP FOR TODAY

Open the bidding pre-emptively whenever you can. What is bad for the enemy must be good for your side.

9. When Opponents Open

Half the time the bidding will be opened by your opponents. This does not mean that you have to keep silent, but you should understand the risk involved in entering the bidding when the opponent on your right has declared his strength. If you make an overcall on a flimsy suit you may find yourself sandwiched between two strong hands. Then the double on your left will be heard two blocks away, and the resulting penalty may run into four figures.

An overcall should be made only if you have a substantial suit capable of producing four or five tricks without any help from partner. Paradoxically, you may overcall on a hand that lacks the high-card strength for an opening bid if your suit is good. Suppose that one club is opened on your right and you hold:

♠: A Q J 10 7
♡: 8 6 3
◇: J 10 4 2
♣: 6

There are several ways in which an overcall of one spade may gain, even if the opponents have the stronger hands.

1 You indicate a good lead for partner if the opponent on your left becomes the declarer.

2 By using up space you may upset your opponents' bidding machinery

and cause them to miss their best contract. Your opponent on the left cannot now bid one heart, for instance, and he may not have the strength to bid two hearts.

3 If you find partner with spade support you may be able to outbid the opponents at the game level. It is worth while losing two or three hundred points in four spades doubled to prevent an enemy game.

In considering an overcall you will naturally be influenced by the vulnerability. To restrict your maximum loss to 500 points, you should be within two tricks of your contract when vulnerable and within three tricks when not vulnerable.

♠ : 7
♡ : A J 5
♢ : 9 6 3
♣ : K Q J 10 8 3

This hand is worth an overcall of two clubs whether you are vulnerable or not.

When Not to Overcall

Many hands that qualify for an opening bid do not contain the material for an overcall. Suppose one heart is opened on your right:

a) ♠ : K J 4   b) ♠ : 7
    ♡ : A 8 3   ♡ : Q J 9 3
    ♢ : 9 8 2   ♢ : A Q 6
    ♣ : A Q 6 2   ♣ : K J 8 5 2

On hand (a) you have a balanced 14-count and no decent suit to bid. You should pass.

On (b) the club suit is too ragged for an overcall, which could be severely punished by a double. When you have length and strength in the enemy suit, as in this case, the sensible course is to pass and hope that the opponents get into trouble.

Responding to Overcalls

Since an overcall does not promise a great deal in the way of high card strength, you need not strain to keep the bidding open. Lacking support for partner's suit, you may pass with as many as 10 points. Raise freely when you have three-card trump support, however. Partner will have at least five cards in his suit.

Suppose your left-hand opponent opens one heart, partner overcalls one spade and the next player passes:

a) ♠: 10 9 3　　b) ♠: Q 8 6　　c) ♠: 9 7 6 2
　 ♡: 8 7 6 4　　　 ♡: A 9 6 2　　　 ♡: 5
　 ◇: A K J 5　　　 ◇: 4　　　　　　 ◇: A K 8 5
　 ♣: 9 5　　　　　 ♣: K Q 7 6 3　　 ♣: A Q 6 4

　 Raise to 2 ♠　　 Raise to 3 ♠　　 Raise to 4 ♠

Jump Overcalls

When you have a strong hand with a good six-card or longer suit, a jump overcall is the right move. After an opening bid of one heart on your right, for instance:

a) ♠: A Q J 8 7 3　　b) ♠: A K
　 ♡: A 6　　　　　　　 ♡: 5
　 ◇: K Q 3　　　　　　 ◇: K Q J 8 6 5 2
　 ♣: 8 4　　　　　　　 ♣: K 9 4

　 Bid 2 ♠　　　　　　　 Bid 3 ◇

The jump overcall is not forcing, but partner should respond with the values for a response to an opening bid.

Note that it is a single jump that shows a strong hand. A double jump is our old friend the pre-emptive bid again.

♠: K Q 10 9 8 6 3
♡: 5
◇: 9 5
♣: Q J 3

Jump to three spades over an opening bid of one in a suit.

Overcall of 1 NT

This indicates the same sort of hand on which you would open the bidding with one no trump, a balanced hand of 15–17 points. Naturally you should have a good stopper (preferably a double stopper) in the enemy suit. Suppose one spade is opened on your right:

♠: A J 9
♡: K 5
◇: K Q J 9 4
♣: Q 9 5

On this hand an overcall of one no trump gives a better picture of your values than a bid of two diamonds.

Partner responds to this overcall exactly as he would to an opening bid of one no trump.

The Take-out Double

This conventional double is an alternative way of entering the auction. The double of an opening bid of one in a suit does not carry the natural meaning that you expect to defeat the contract. Instead, the message is: 'Partner, I have a fair hand with support for each of the other three suits. Kindly name your longest suit.'

Suppose that one diamond is opened on your right:

a) ♠: Q J 7 4   b) ♠: K Q 6   c) ♠: A J 9 5 3
   ♡: A Q 8 6   ♡: A J 9 3   ♡: Q 6 5 2
   ◇: 2   ◇: 8 4   ◇: 5
   ♣: K 10 6 3   ♣: A 9 8 2   ♣: A K 8

In each case you should double to ask for partner's best suit. You have support for anything he may bid, and it is clearly desirable to give him a choice rather than embark on a guessing game of your own. In effect, the take-out double bids three suits at once.

The minimum strength for a take-out double is about 12 points with shortage in the enemy suit.

When is a Double for Take-Out?

The double of a suit bid is regarded as conventional only when the doubler's partner has not made a bid. If partner has said anything other than 'no bid', your double will be interpreted as a penalty double and will not be taken out. We shall shortly be taking a look at penalty doubles, but meanwhile remember that you cannot double for take-out after partner has bid.

Responding to a Double

When partner makes a take-out double and the next player passes, you are expected to bid your best suit no matter how weak your hand. A minimum response promises nothing more than four cards in the suit. Suppose one heart is opened on your left, partner doubles and the next player passes:

a) ♠: 9 7 6 2   b) ♠: 9 4   c) ♠: K J 10 6 5
   ♡: 7 6 4   ♡: 10 5 3   ♡: 4 3
   ◇: J 8 4 2   ◇: Q 4 2   ◇: 8 5
   ♣: 6 3   ♣: 10 8 7 3 2   ♣: A 7 4 3

  Bid 1 ♠   Bid 2 ♣   Bid 2 ♠

On weak hands such as (a) and (b) you make the cheapest possible bid. Hand (c) contains 8 points and a good major suit, and you must not make the same bid as on hand (a). Jump to indicate the extra values.

One no trump is the response on a balanced hand with 6–9 points and stoppers in the enemy suit. When you have real length and strength in the doubled suit you may consider a penalty pass. Assuming the same start to the auction, 1 ♡ — double — pass:

d) ♠: 4 3 2   e) ♠: 6 4
   ♡: K J 9 3   ♡: Q J 10 9 7 6
   ◇: Q 7 4   ◇: 5 3
   ♣: 9 6 2   ♣: K 8 5

   Bid 1 NT   Pass

With a good double stopper in hearts on hand (d), one no trump is the bid. Hand (e) is the sort of hand that justifies a pass. With four probable trump tricks, you are happy to defend against one heart doubled.

When the next player bids over your partner's double, you are relieved of the duty of finding a response on a weak hand. A voluntary response therefore shows some values — perhaps 5 or 6 points and a five-card suit.

Counter to Take-Out Double

Let us change seats for a moment and consider the action that should be taken when partner's opening bid is doubled for take-out.

In this situation all raises are defensive in nature, aimed at preventing the opponents from reaching their best contract. Suppose partner opens one spade and the next player doubles:

a) ♠: J 10 6 3   b) ♠: K J 8 3   c) ♠: Q J 8 6 3
   ♡: 5   ♡: 5   ♡: 5
   ◇: Q 8 7 2   ◇: Q J 10 5   ◇: K 10 8 7 2
   ♣: 10 7 5 2   ♣: 10 7 5 2   ♣: 10 5

   Raise to 2 ♠   Raise to 3 ♠   Raise to 4 ♠

The bid of a new suit is no longer forcing, but shows a good, playable suit. The response of one no trump is restricted to the upper range of 8–9 points.

d) ♠: 7   e) ♠: 9 5
   ♡: 10 6 4   ♡: J 10 4 3
   ◇: 7 6 5   ◇: K 8 4
   ♣: K Q 10 9 7 2   ♣: A 10 5 2

   Bid 2 ♣   Bid 1 NT

With any strong hand you should counter with a redouble. This promises 10 or more points, giving partner the glad news that your side has the better hands. You can expect either to make a contract of your own or to double the opponents for a juicy penalty.

When you redouble, you may or may not have trump support for partner. After one spade from partner and a double on your right:

f) ♠: A 10 7 5   g) ♠: J 6
  ♡: K 6   ♡: K J 9 2
  ◇: K Q 6 5   ◇: Q 10 7 4
  ♣: 9 5 3   ♣: A 9 7

  Redouble   Redouble

You do not expect to play in one spade redoubled, but if it happens you need shed no tears. When the contract is made it will give you game (4 x 30 = 120). More likely, however, the opponents will run from the redouble by bidding one of their suits, whereupon you can either try for a penalty by doubling or try for a game of your own.

Penalty Doubles

By definition, a take-out double is the double of a *suit* before partner has bid. The double of an enemy bid of one no trump does not come into this category. It is a penalty or 'business' double. For a successful double of an opening bid of one no trump, your hand needs to be rather stronger than that of the opening bidder.

♠: A 7
♡: Q 8 4
◇: K Q J 10 3
♣: A Q 4

When one no trump is opened on your right, you can double on this hand with a good expectancy of defeating the contract. You trust your partner to pass on any balanced hand. The more strength he has, the better your penalty will be. If partner has a hopeless hand with a long suit, however, he may take out the double by bidding two in his suit.

Opportunities for some of the most lucrative penalty doubles occur on the first round of bidding, when partner's opening bid is overcalled by an unwary opponent. You start with the advantage of knowing that your partner will provide two or three tricks in defence. If you have a poor fit in partner's suit, a good fit in the opponent's suit and a couple of defensive tricks on the side, you may be able to chastise the enemy severely. Suppose that partner opens one spade and the next player comes in with two clubs:

a) ♠: Q 5   b) ♠: 2   c) ♠: 10 9 4
  ♡: A 10 4   ♡: K 8 6 3   ♡: A 7 3
  ◇: Q 8 7 2   ◇: A J 5 2   ◇: K 9 5 4
  ♣: K J 9 3   ♣: Q 10 7 4   ♣: K J 3

  Double   Double   Bid 2 NT

On hand (a) you expect to make about five tricks plus whatever partner can provide in defence against two clubs. Again on (b) the double stands out. The fewer cards you hold in partner's suit, the better your defensive prospects. On (c) you have too many spades and too few clubs to make the double an attractive proposition. Prefer the natural response of two no trumps.

Doubles of higher contracts are seldom as profitable, since opponents do not generally bid high without good values. Do not double a freely bid game or slam unless you have a surprise for the declarer in the form of sure trump tricks.

TIP FOR TODAY

Overcall boldly when you are short in
the enemy suit, but keep quiet when
you have length.

10. Basic Card Play

Reaching the right contract is only half the battle at this game. If you are to achieve anything at all you must also learn how to make the most of your cards. In this chapter we shall examine the elements of winning card play.

How Tricks Are Won

Anyone can win a trick with an ace, but you will not score enough tricks for your contract simply by cashing aces. There are not enough of them in the pack. Extra tricks have to be developed by establishing lower cards as winners. Suppose that you hold a number of cards in sequence in one suit.

a) K Q J 10   b) Q J 10 9   c) J 10 9 8

There is no immediate winner in any of these holdings, but in (a) you can lead the king to drive out the enemy ace. When the ace has gone, you will make three tricks in the suit with your queen, jack and ten. This is the principle of promotion at work. When a high honour card in a suit is played, every lower card is promoted one step in rank. When two high cards go on the same trick, the lower cards are promoted two positions in rank. When the king drives out the ace, the queen is promoted from third to first rank and controls the next round of the suit.

Similarly in (b), two tricks can be established for the ten and nine after the queen and jack have forced out the opposing ace and king. And in (c), given time, a trick can be established by driving out the ace, king and queen.

A spectacular illustration of promotion is seen in the next diagram.

K 6 4 3

Q   A 7 5 2

J 10 9 8

The declarer's lead of the jack is covered by the queen, king and ace. What has happened? Four high cards have been used on the first round, and the ten receives a giant boost from fifth rank to first. With the nine and the eight enjoying similar promotion, the declarer wins the next three tricks in the suit.

Small cards may also be established as winners, but it is clear that the two—thirteenth in rank—can become a winner only when all the other cards of the suit have been played.

8 7 5

J 9 3   10 6 4

A K Q 2

Here you can play the ace, king and queen in succession. When the adverse cards divide evenly, your two becomes established and will win a fourth trick for you.

The longer your suit, the better your chance of establishing the small cards.

6 5

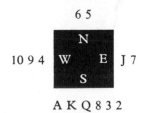

10 9 4   J 7

A K Q 8 3 2

In this case the ace, king and queen suffice to draw all the enemy cards, leaving you with three further winners in the suit.

In a very short suit, you have no chance of making extra tricks with your small cards.

7 6 3

A K 8

Only the defenders can establish extra tricks in a suit like this. The declarer should therefore leave such holdings strictly alone while he attempts to establish tricks elsewhere. It is a common mistake for beginners to cash their aces and kings prematurely. They should be retained as long as possible, for they serve to prevent the opponents from establishing early tricks in the suit. The play of the hand in no trump contracts is rather like a race in which each side tries to establish winners by knocking out the enemy stoppers.

Handling Your Winners

If you have a number of top cards in sequence in your own hand, the order in which you play them is unimportant. Holding A K Q J, for instance, you need not play the ace first. Since you have the only three higher cards, the jack will win the first trick just as well as the ace. In a sense, your cards are all equals, and you can play them in any order you like.

Care is needed, however, when the top cards are divided between your hand and dummy.

K 5

A Q J 3

Again four tricks can be made without trouble — but only if you play the cards in a certain order. Suppose you cash the ace first, and then lead the three to dummy's king. It will be dummy's turn to lead, and there may be no way of returning to your hand to cash the other two tricks in the suit. This blockage can be easily avoided by leading the three and winning the first round of the suit with the king. The second, third and fourth rounds can then be won by the ace, queen and jack in any order.

Here is a general rule to follow. When high cards touching in rank are divided between the two hands, play first the high cards from the shorter holding. This makes for smooth communication.

The principle is exactly the same if the ace is missing.

J 10 6 5

K Q 4

Tackle the suit by leading the king and continuing with the queen. If the ace wins the first or second trick, you will be able to lead the four and win two more tricks with the jack and ten.

Leading up to High Cards

When your high cards are not in sequence, your best chance of making tricks lies in leading from the weaker hand towards the stronger. Look at this example.

A Q

K 3   9 7

8 5

If you lead from the North hand there is no chance of making more than one trick. The ace will win the first round, but West will play the three, retaining his king to capture the queen on the next round.

See the difference if you lead from the South hand. West is helpless because he has to play ahead of North. If West plays the king you can capture it with the ace and score a second trick with the queen. In practice West is likely to play the three, but now you can insert the queen from the North hand and win two tricks anyway.

The attempt to win a trick with a card that is lower in rank than the highest enemy card is called a finesse. It is one of the commonest plays in the game. Finesses do not always succeed but they have a fifty-fifty chance, depending on the favourable position of the missing honour card. In the last example the finesse must fail if East has the king instead of West. But you have nothing to lose by trying it.

Here are some more finessing positions.

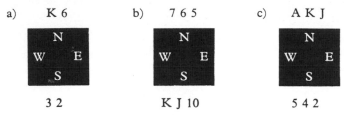

a) K 6   b) 7 6 5   c) A K J

3 2   K J 10   5 4 2

In diagram (a) there is no chance of winning a trick by leading from the North hand. But if you lead from South towards the king you can make a trick whenever the ace is with West.

In (b) the high cards are in the South hand and you should therefore lead from North, playing the ten if East follows with a low card. This time you are hoping to find the queen with East, in which case you will make two tricks in the suit. The position of the ace is immaterial. You must lose a trick to the ace anyway.

Diagram (c) illustrates another finesse against the queen. Lead from the South hand and try the jack if West plays low. Half the time you will make three tricks in the suit.

When you have a number of honour cards in sequence, you may be able to catch an enemy card in a pincer movement and avoid the loss of a trick.

A 7 5 4

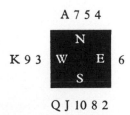

K 9 3   6

Q J 10 8 2

Lead the queen, and play low from dummy unless West covers with the king. Continue with the jack and repeat the process. As soon as the king appears, you can kill it with the ace and run the suit without loss. The fate of your contract will often depend on the success or failure of a finesse of this sort.

Do not lead an honour card for a finesse unless you can afford to have it covered by the enemy honour.

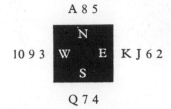

In this situation there is no point in leading the queen from the South hand. If West had the king he would play it on the queen, and you would be restricted to one trick in the suit. The way to try for two tricks is to lead a low card to the ace and lead back towards your queen. This nets two tricks whenever East has the king.

Finessing is also profitable for the defenders, who have an advantage in that they can see the finesse is going to succeed.

Suppose that West leads the two and the seven is played from dummy. Now it would be wasteful for East to play the ace. Since the king is in dummy and has not been played, the queen is high enough to win the first trick. The ace captures the king on the second round, and West takes the next two tricks with his jack and nine.

There are many other finessing positions which you will meet in due course. You will not go far wrong if you remember the basic principle of leading from the weaker hand towards the stronger.

Covering an Honour

A problem peculiar to the defending side arises when the declarer leads an honour card in a finessing situation. Usually it is right for the next player to cover with a higher honour if he has one. The principle of promotion supplies the reason. By forcing the declarer to use two honour cards to win one trick, the defender expects to promote lower cards in his hand to winning rank.

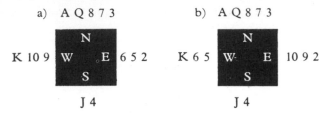

a)   A Q 8 7 3

K 10 9   W   E   6 5 2

J 4

b)   A Q 8 7 3

K 6 5   W   E   10 9 2

J 4

In each case South leads the jack. If West plays low, so will dummy, and the declarer will finesse the queen on the second round to make all five tricks in the suit.

In diagram (a) West should see that he can promote a trick for his ten by covering the jack with his king. The ace wins the first trick, the queen takes the second, and the ten is a winner on the third round of the suit.

The position is not so obvious in (b) since West does not have the ten himself, but he has nothing to lose by covering the jack with his king. Once again this promotes a trick for the ten on the third round.

There is no difference when the lead comes from dummy.

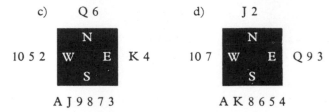

c)   Q 6

10 5 2   W   E   K 4

A J 9 8 7 3

d)   J 2

10 7   W   E   Q 9 3

A K 8 6 5 4

In diagram (c) East should cover the queen with his king on the chance of promoting a card in his partner's hand. Likewise, in (d) East should cover the jack with his queen. When the ten appears on the second round the nine is promoted to winning rank.

When Not to Cover

Remember that the sole purpose of covering honours is to promote your intermediate cards. Do not cover when there can be nothing to promote.

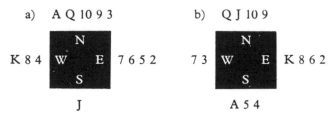

a)   A Q 10 9 3

K 8 4   W   E   7 6 5 2

J

b)   Q J 10 9

7 3   W   E   K 8 6 2

A 5 4

In diagram (a) there is no point in covering with the king when the jack is led. Dummy has such good cards that there can be nothing to promote in partner's hand. Play low in the hope that the jack is a singleton, in which case your king will be worth a trick after all.

Similarly in diagram (b), the solid sequence in dummy tells you that there are no promotional prospects. To cover with the king when the queen is led would simply give the declarer four tricks in the suit instead of three.

Do not cover when it may cost you a trick.

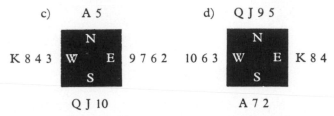

c)   A 5   d)   Q J 9 5

K 8 4 3   9 7 6 2   10 6 3   K 8 4

Q J 10   A 7 2

In (c) it would be unwise for West to cover when the queen is led. Since dummy has only two cards in the suit, the king cannot be caught. The declarer is held to two tricks if West plays low, but he makes three if West covers.

Do you see what may happen in diagram (d) if East covers the queen with his king? On winning with the ace the declarer will be in a position to lead towards dummy and finesse the nine, thus losing no trick in the suit. In order to avoid this disaster, East should play low when the queen is led from dummy but cover with the king if the declarer continues with the jack.

This is usually the correct procedure when an honour card is led from two honours in sequence. The defender should play low when the first honour is led, but cover the second one.

The Duck

Returning to the subject of developing extra tricks from small cards, let us consider the position below.

A K 8 5 3

Q 9 2   J 10

7 6 4

Assume that you need to develop tricks in this suit, and that dummy has no high cards in the other suits. If you cash the ace and king of the suit and continue with a third round, all the enemy cards will be removed and the two remaining small cards in dummy will be winners. But winners are useless if there is no means of reaching them, and dummy has no other high cards.

How can you organize the play so as to enjoy the extra winners that are rightfully yours? The solution is simple once you think of it. You can overcome the communication problem by 'ducking' on the first round, playing low from both hands and allowing the opponents to win the trick. This costs nothing, for the defenders are bound to make a trick in the suit anyway. All you are doing is conceding it on the first round instead of the third. And that is worth two extra tricks. When you regain the lead, your play of the ace and king removes all the enemy cards, and the lead remains in dummy for you to cash the established small cards.

I know that it may not be easy for you to appreciate the value of conceding an early trick to the opponents. Beginners tend to hang on to the lead as long as possible, fearing that the defenders may do something diabolical when they get in. But it is a fact that in most contracts you will have to surrender the lead several times. The timing can be all-important. One of the big secrets of winning play is to give the opponents the tricks they are bound to make as quickly as possible.

It has been said that the difference between a beginner and an expert playing a contract of three no trumps is that the beginner makes eight tricks early while the expert makes nine tricks late. Why not start like an expert by letting your opponents have their tricks first?

The duck may be repeated in certain cases.

A 7 6 5 3

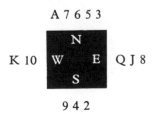

K 10   Q J 8

9 4 2

Needing three tricks from this suit with no other high cards in dummy, you can succeed only by ducking twice. Play low from both hands on the first round. When you regain the lead, play another low card from each hand. That gives the defenders two tricks in the suit, but you will make the remainder. When you come in again, lead your third card and play dummy's ace. That draws the last enemy card in the suit, and the lead is in the right place for you to score the established small cards.

The strategem of conceding the first trick in a suit is often employed by the defenders. We do not say that a defender ducks in making an opening lead, but the principle is exactly the same.

J 8 4

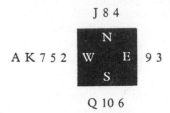

A K 7 5 2   9 3

Q 10 6

Defending against a no trump contract, West should lead a small card, not the ace or the king. This allows the declarer to win the first round, but if East can regain the lead at any stage he will be able to lead his second card and give his partner four tricks in the suit.

Try it from the East seat.

Q J 10

8 5   A K 9 6 2

7 4 3

West leads the eight against a no trump contract and the queen is played from dummy. Yes, of course, East should duck in order to preserve communication with his partner.

The Hold-Up

When you play the hand in a no trump contract, the defenders will normally attack in their long suit, trying to establish extra tricks for themselves. You should not allow your stoppers to be forced out too easily.

10 5

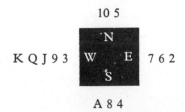

K Q J 9 3   7 6 2

A 8 4

When West leads the king, for instance, your instincts may tell you to clobber it with the ace. Fight against such instincts. If you take your ace at once, the defenders will be in a position to run four tricks in the suit as soon as either of them gains the lead. Instead you should 'hold up' your ace, playing a low card and allowing West to win the trick. When he continues with the queen you should hold up again, keeping your ace for the third round.

Do you see the difference this may make ? The point is that West may have no way of gaining the lead in another suit, and when you surrender a trick to East he will have no means of passing the lead across to his partner. Thus instead of losing four tricks in the suit you may lose only two.

Superficially the hold-up looks very much like the duck. The common denominator is the concession to an opponent of a trick which you might have won yourself. The two plays have different purposes, however. In the duck your objective is to preserve your own lines of communication, while in the hold-up you are out to cut the enemy communications by exhausting the holding of one opponent.

The hold-up can be equally useful in defence.

K J 10 7 4

8 2   A 6 5

Q 9 3

If dummy has no high cards elsewhere, East can prevent the declarer from enjoying more than two tricks in the suit by holding up his ace until the third round.

TIP FOR TODAY

Try to develop extra tricks before
releasing your aces and kings.

11. Declarer's Play

The time has come to consider the play of a complete hand. Problems are compounded when you have four suits to think about. The right play in any particular suit may turn out to be the wrong play for the hand as a whole.

When the opening lead is made and dummy is spread out on the table, the first thing you should do is sit back and take a cool look at your combined resources. Do not play a card until you have formed a plan. Count your quick winners (the tricks you can make without losing the lead), calculate how many extra tricks you need to develop, and decide which suit is most likely to provide those extra tricks.

No Trump Contracts

The defenders will normally attack in their long suit, and you have to rely on your high cards to control the situation. Your aim must be to develop enough extra tricks in your own long suits before the defenders can establish and run their suit.

♠: A

♡: A Q 3

◇: K Q 10 8 3

♣: Q 7 4 2

You play in three no trumps on a spade lead. A count of quick winners gives a total of five, two in spades and three in hearts. Four extra tricks must therefore be developed to fulfil your contract.

♠: K 8 5

♡: K 9 7

◇: J 5 4

♣: K J 10 6

There are chances for extra tricks in clubs and diamonds, but you will not have time to develop both suits. When you surrender the lead to the defenders they will drive out your remaining spade stopper, and they will be able to run at least three spade tricks to defeat the contract if they ever get in again. You must therefore plan to establish all the tricks you need in one suit. That lets clubs out, for the suit will provide no more than three tricks after the defenders have taken their ace. It should be possible to develop four tricks in diamonds, however, since dummy has five cards in the suit.

Having made your plan, you win the first trick with the ace of spades and lead a low diamond to your jack (first the high cards from the shorter holding, remember). After knocking out the ace of diamonds you are assured of nine tricks — four diamonds, three hearts and two spades.

Your contract is again three no trumps in the next hand, and West attacks your weak spot by leading a heart.

♠ : K 8 6 5
♡ : 4
♢ : 10 7 6 4
♣ : A J 10 9

♠ : A Q 7
♡ : A K
♢ : Q J 9 8 3
♣ : Q 7 2

This time you can count six quick winners, leaving three additional tricks to be developed. Given time, you could establish three tricks in diamonds, your longest combined suit. But time is the one thing you do not have. The initial heart lead has put the defenders a tempo ahead, and they will set up enough heart tricks to defeat the contract before you can establish your diamonds. You must therefore look elsewhere for your tricks.

The other possibility is the club suit. If the king of clubs is with West, you should be able to make four tricks in the suit by finessing. After winning the first heart trick you should lead the queen of clubs, playing low from dummy unless West produces the king. If the queen wins, continue with another club and finesse dummy's ten. Then return to hand with a spade and take a third finesse.

Even if the club finesse fails and a heart is returned, you are not without hope. Discard a diamond from dummy on the second heart, play the rest of the clubs, and then turn to the spades. Lead a low spade to your ace, cash the queen of spades (high cards from the short holding first), and continue with your third spade to the king. If the enemy spades are divided 3–3, dummy's last spade will provide your ninth trick.

Watch the Entries

When you can win a trick in either hand, preserve the winner in the hand that is most likely to need a card of entry later in the play. Here is a common situation. The contract is two no trumps and West leads the ten of diamonds.

♠ : 9 6 5
♡ : J 5 4
♢ : K 6
♣ : K J 10 9 3

♠ : A 10 7 3
♡ : A 7 6 2
♢ : A J
♣ : Q 6 2

The success or failure of the contract hangs on your play to the first trick.

You can count four quick winners and you need to develop four more tricks from the club suit. If you win the first trick in dummy with the king of diamonds, a defender may be able to defeat you by holding up his ace of clubs until the third round of the suit. Then you will have no way of reaching dummy to enjoy the established club tricks.

The correct play at trick one is the six of diamonds from dummy and the ace from your hand. Don't be tempted to win a 'cheap' trick with the jack of diamonds. You must play the ace in order to guarantee a later entry to dummy. Then you can tackle the clubs, first leading the queen from your hand, with no worries about a possible hold-up of the ace. Eventually you will be able to cross to dummy by leading your jack of diamonds to the king, and you cannot be prevented from making eight tricks.

Many holdings can be manipulated to provide entries where they are most needed. Here is an example.

A Q 10

K J 2

Depending on the needs of the situation, the declarer can win one, two or all three tricks in the North hand. It is a useful exercise to work out for yourself how this is achieved.

When there are no entry cards in the outside suits, you may have to resort to a duck. On the next hand West leads a spade against your contract of three no trumps. East wins with the ace and returns a spade to dummy's queen.

♠: Q J
♡: K 8 3
♢: A K 9 6 5 4
♣: 8 5

N
W   E
S

♠: K 7 5
♡: Q J 5
♢: 7 2
♣: A K 6 4 3

Two spades, two diamonds and two clubs give you a total of six quick winners, leaving three more to be established. Neither hearts nor clubs offer a chance of the three extra tricks you need, but diamonds will provide them if the adverse cards divide 3–2.

You could play the ace, king and another diamond, but then you would be unable to reach the established winners since dummy has no quick entry card in the other suits. As we saw in the last chapter, the way to preserve communication is to duck the first round of diamonds. At trick three lead the four of diamonds from the table, allowing the opponents to win the trick. No matter what they return, you will then be able to reach dummy by leading your second diamond. Five diamond tricks, two spades and two clubs will give you the contract if diamonds do, in fact, break 3–2.

Your contract is again three no trumps, and West leads a low spade to his partner's king.

♠: 9 3
♡: K 10 5
◇: A 10 9 6 5
♣: 8 6 3

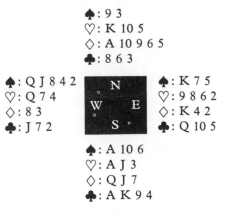

♠: A 10 6
♡: A J 3
◇: Q J 7
♣: A K 9 4

Again you have six top winners and need to develop three additional tricks. The diamond position is promising. A finesse will produce four extra tricks if West has the king.

Is your contract then totally dependent on the success of the diamond finesse? By no means. Since three extra tricks are all you need, you can afford a losing diamond finesse provided that you lose no more than three spade tricks.

One favourable possibility is that the spades are divided 4–4. And on this type of hand you can also guard against a long spade suit in the West hand by the use of hold-up play.

Allow East to win the first trick, playing the six of spades from your hand. When spades are continued play the ten, giving the opponents a second trick. On winning the third spade you can take an immediate diamond finesse, and you will make your contract (a) when West has the king of diamonds and (b) when East has the king of diamonds but no more than four spades. The complete deal may be:

♠: 9 3
♡: K 10 5
◇: A 10 9 6 5
♣: 8 6 3

♠: Q J 8 4 2   ♠: K 7 5
♡: Q 7 4   ♡: 9 8 6 2
◇: 8 3   ◇: K 4 2
♣: J 7 2   ♣: Q 10 5

♠: A 10 6
♡: A J 3
◇: Q J 7
♣: A K 9 4

Be sure that you appreciate what will happen if you play your ace on the first or second round of spades. The defenders will make crowing noises and five tricks.

Placing the Lead

On the last hand the winning technique was to hold up an ace until one defender was incapable of making a damaging return. It frequently happens that one particular defender is in a position to endanger your contract while the other is not. In such cases you must try to concede tricks only to the defender who is harmless.

West leads a low heart against your contract of three no trumps and East plays the jack.

♠: K Q 4
♡: 8 5
◇: A K 10 7
♣: K J 5 3

♠: A 10 8
♡: K Q 6
◇: 9 4 3
♣: A 10 6 2

After taking the first trick you can count no fewer than eight quick winners. And the club suit should provide the extra trick you need, even if a trick has to be lost to the queen.

Your club holding is such that you can finesse against the queen in either direction. You can lead the ace and continue with the two, playing the jack from dummy unless the queen appears, or you can start by leading the two of clubs to the king and return the three for a finesse of the ten. Which way is better?

The question must be considered within the context of the whole hand, and that means giving a little thought to the heart position. West might well have a long heart suit headed by the ace and ten, in which case it would be highly dangerous to allow East to gain the lead. A heart return from East might enable his partner to run four or five tricks in the suit. In contrast, West is harmless on lead, for he cannot continue the heart attack without allowing you to score a second trick in the suit.

Now it is clear how the clubs should be played. You should lead the two of clubs to the king and return the three, playing the ten from hand unless the queen appears. You do not care if this finesse wins or loses. Either way your contract is completely safe.

Suit Contracts

One of the main advantages of playing in a trump suit is that you enjoy an extra degree of control. There is not the same need to rely on high cards to stop the run of an enemy suit. Your trumps will do the job for you.

Here is a typical trump contract. You are in four hearts, and West leads the king of diamonds followed by the queen.

♠ : K 9 4 3
♡ : Q 6
◇ : 9 7 5
♣ : A Q J 4

♠ : A 8 5
♡ : K J 10 5 4 2
◇ : 6
♣ : K 8 3

You are able to trump the second diamond with the two of hearts, thus restricting the defenders to one trick in diamonds.

The correct move at the next trick is a low trump to dummy's queen. Your aim should be to extract the small trumps held by the enemy as soon as possible. Remember that while you can use your small trumps to kill the defenders' high cards, they can do exactly the same to you. On most hands it is right, therefore, to assign top priority to 'drawing trumps'. That is why it is so important to choose a trump suit in which your side has numerical superiority.

Ideally, you want to have a trump or two left over after drawing the enemy trumps.

On this hand you should knock out the ace of hearts, trump the diamond return, and draw the remaining trumps. Only then is it safe for you to cash your winners in clubs and spades. Barring accidents, you should wind up with eleven tricks — five trumps, two spades and four clubs.

Apart from the extra control it confers, a trump suit often enables you to develop extra tricks by trumping losing cards in the shorter trump hand. When you need to develop tricks in this way you may have to postpone the drawing of the enemy trumps.

West leads the two of diamonds against your contract of four spades.

♠: Q 7 5 4
♡: 3
♢: A J 8 5
♣: Q 7 6 2

♠: A K J 10 6
♡: A 9 4
♢: Q 4 3
♣: J 8

Your top winners are five spades and the two red aces. A second trick can be established in diamonds, however, and two extra tricks can be made by ruffing (another word for trumping) your losing hearts with dummy's spades. Your only losers, in fact, should be one diamond and two clubs.

It may be tempting to take the diamond finesse by playing low from dummy at the first trick, but there is danger in this course. The two of diamonds may be a singleton, in which case East will win with the king and return a diamond for his partner to ruff.

East may then be able to regain the lead in clubs and play another diamond, and the defence may win the first five tricks. It would be humiliating to go down in an easy contract through greed for an overtrick. It is the making of the contract that matters. Overtricks are relatively unimportant, and you should not take an unnecessary finesse.

Play the ace of diamonds on the first trick and lead the three of hearts to your ace. Trump your second heart in dummy with the four of spades, lead the five of spades to your ten, and ruff the third heart with the queen of spades. Return to hand by leading the seven of spades to your jack, draw any trumps that are still outstanding, and then lead the queen of diamonds, forcing out the king and establishing your tenth trick.

At times you will have to give up a trick in a suit before you can make use of the power of dummy's trumps.

Against your contract of four hearts, West leads the king of diamonds followed by the queen. He then switches to a trump, which you win in hand with the ten.

♠: 8 4
♡: K 5 2
◇: 9 7 5 4
♣: K 9 6 3

Six trumps, two clubs and a spade give you a total of nine top winners. You have lost two diamond tricks already, and you have two potential losers in spades. What is to be done about it?

Dummy's shortage in spades provides the answer. You will be able to trump one of your losing spades in dummy provided that you tackle the preparatory work without delay. Play the ace of spades and continue with a small one, conceding the trick to the defenders. You can win a trump return in hand and lead your third spade, ruffing in dummy with the king of hearts. Return to hand with the ace of clubs, draw any trump that is still out, and the rest of the tricks are yours.

♠: A 9 3
♡: A Q J 10 7 6
◇: 8 2
♣: A 5

Note that it would be unsound to draw a second round of trumps before playing spades. It makes no difference when the opposing trumps break 2–2, but the more likely distribution is 3–1. In the latter case, on gaining the lead with the second spade, a defender might be able to lead a third trump, removing the last trump from dummy and leaving you with no means of disposing of your losing spade.

Establishing a Side-Suit by Trumping

In general, you can create an extra trump trick only by ruffing a loser in the shorter trump hand. Ruffing in the longer trump hand does not gain a trick, for you expect to make the long trumps anyway. However, the trumps in the long hand are often used to facilitate the establishment of a side-suit in dummy. If the trumps in dummy are needed as entry cards, you may again have to delay the drawing of trumps.

On the next hand your contract is five diamonds. West leads the king of hearts and continues with a small heart to his partner's ace. East returns the ten of spades which you win with the ace.

♠ : 7 5 4
♡ : 8 3
◊ : Q J 4
♣ : A 9 6 5 3

For quick winners you have six trumps and two tricks in each of the black suits. You could, of course, draw trumps and rely on a finesse against the queen of spades for your eleventh trick.

But a better plan is to try to establish the long club suit in dummy. This will succeed if neither opponent has more than four clubs or more than three trumps.

♠ : A K J
♡ : 9 7
◊ : A K 10 6 5 2
♣ : K 7

Dummy's trumps are needed as entries, so you cannot afford to draw more than one round of trumps immediately. First cash the ace of trumps to test the position. If either opponent is void, you will have to draw the remaining trumps and fall back upon the spade finesse. But if both defenders play a trump, you can proceed with the plan to establish the club suit.

Play the king of clubs and continue with the seven to dummy's ace. Lead a third club and trump it with your ten of diamonds (ruffing high to avoid an over-ruff if West has no more clubs). Cross to dummy by leading a low diamond to the jack, and lead a fourth club, trumping with the king of diamonds. By this time all the opposing clubs will have gone, even if the division was 4–2, and dummy's nine will be a master. Lead a low trump to the queen, drawing any outstanding trump in the process, and discard your jack of spades on the established club winner. Eleven tricks are thus made without risking the spade finesse.

The full hand may be as follows:

♠ : 7 5 4
♡ : 8 3
◊ : Q J 4
♣ : A 9 6 5 3

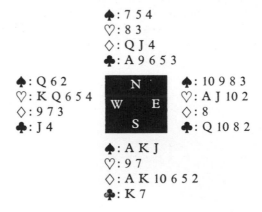

♠ : Q 6 2
♡ : K Q 6 5 4
◊ : 9 7 3
♣ : J 4

♠ : 10 9 8 3
♡ : A J 10 2
◊ : 8
♣ : Q 10 8 2

♠ : A K J
♡ : 9 7
◊ : A K 10 6 5 2
♣ : K 7

Going for a Quick Discard

Another occasion for postponing the drawing of trumps is when there is a more urgent job to be done. On the next hand your contract is four spades and West leads the queen of hearts.

♠: Q 10 8 6
♡: A 8 3
♢: Q 5
♣: K J 10 3

There are only two quick winners, but you should be able to develop three tricks in spades, two in diamonds and three in clubs to bring your total up to the required ten. The position is not so healthy if you count losers, however. There are three aces to lose, and the attack in hearts threatens to establish a fourth trick for the defenders in that suit.

♠: K J 9 4
♡: K 5 2
♢: K J 7
♣: Q 8 4

Clearly you cannot afford to play trumps immediately. When in with the ace of spades the defenders would knock out your second heart stopper, and as soon as they regained the lead they would cash their heart trick.

There is no time to lose. You must find a way of discarding a losing heart from one hand or the other before the opponents can cash a trick in the suit. Clubs are hopeless, for you cannot enjoy a discard on the fourth club until trumps have been drawn. But diamonds offer good prospects. If you knock out the ace of diamonds you will later be able to discard the losing heart in dummy on one of your diamonds.

Does it matter whether you win the first heart with the ace or the king? Indeed it does. You may need a quick entry to your hand to enable you to cash the third diamond, so you should win the first trick in dummy with the ace of hearts. Then lead the queen of diamonds (first the high card from the shorter holding). If this is allowed to win, continue with another diamond to force out the ace. You can win the heart return in hand, discard the losing heart in dummy on your master diamond, and at last turn your attention to the trump suit.

The Cross-Ruff

There is one fairly common type of hand on which trumps should not be drawn at all. Instead, you set out to score all your trumps separately by ruffing in both hands. Here is an example.

West leads the ace of clubs against your contract of four hearts.

♠: —
♡: K Q 10 5
◇: J 7 5 3
♣: Q 8 7 3 2

There is only one quick winner outside the trump suit, but with voids in both hands you are ideally placed to make all nine of your trumps separately.

Ruff the opening lead in your hand, ruff a spade in dummy and return to the ace of diamonds. Then ruff spades and clubs alternately until your opponents go cross-eyed. After making the first ten tricks, you can graciously concede the remainder.

♠: K 9 8 4
♡: A J 9 8 3
◇: A 9 4 2
♣: —

When playing a cross-ruff it is advisable to cash any winners you have in the side suits at an early stage. Otherwise the defenders may discard while you are ruffing and eventually ruff your side winners.

Note that the defenders might have done better by leading a trump. That would have forced you to use two of your valuable trumps on the one trick.

TIP FOR TODAY

Stop and think when dummy goes down. Make a plan before playing to the first trick.

12. Defensive Play

In the play of the cards the declarer has the easier task. Not only can he see the strength of the forces at his disposal, but he is in sole command of the play of twenty-six cards. The defenders have to operate without sight of each other's hands and often find it difficult to co-ordinate their efforts.

One compensating advantage is that the defenders have the privilege of making the opening lead. This can be a doubtful privilege at times, for the opening lead has to be made before dummy goes down on the table.

Opening Leads Against No Trumps

Before leading, the defender on the left of the declarer should ask himself a two-fold question.

1 Which suit offers the best chance of defeating the contract?
2 Which card should be led from that suit?

In general, the best plan against a no trump contract is to lead your longest suit in the hope of establishing extra winners. If the suit is headed by three cards in sequence, lead the top card.

from	K Q J 8 3 2	lead the	king
	Q J 10 9		queen
	J 10 9 5 2		jack

From a broken sequence, where the third card in line is missing, the top card is still the right choice.

from	K Q 10 8 5	lead the	king
	Q J 9 4 3 2		queen
	J 10 8 7		jack

An exception arises when your sequence contains the ace and king. Now the king is the normal card to lead.

| from | A K Q 7 5 | lead the | king |
| | A K J 8 | | king |

If you have what is known as an interior sequence, where the second card in line is missing (or the second and third cards), lead the honour card immediately below the gap.

from	A Q J 9 5	lead the	queen
	A J 10 7 2		jack
	K J 10 6 5		jack
	A 10 9 8 2		ten
	K 10 9 7		ten
	Q 10 9 6 3		ten

When you have no sequence, it is conventional to lead the fourth-highest card of your longest suit.

from   K 10 6 2   lead the two
        A K 8 7 3   seven
        K J 9 5 4 2   five

The main purpose of this convention is to help partner to judge how many cards you have in the suit. When you lead the two, for instance, partner knows at once that you have led from a four-card suit. Similarly, if you lead the three and play the two on the next round partner will know that you started with five cards in the suit.

Do not lead the fourth-highest when your suit consists of four small cards, however. It is better to lead the top card, which tells partner that you have no honour cards in the suit.

from   9 8 6 3   lead the nine

Leading Partner's Suit

When your partner has mentioned a suit in the bidding, it is usually right to lead his suit rather than try to establish a long suit of your own.

Lead the top card in partner's suit when you have two honour cards in sequence, two or three small cards, or a doubleton honour.

from   Q J 5   lead the queen
        9 7 3   nine
        6 2   six
        K 6   king

In leading an honour card from a short holding in partner's suit you are following the familiar principle of playing first the high cards from the shorter holding.

6 5 3

K 7   Q J 9 8 4

A 10 2

West's lead of the king facilitates the development of his partner's suit and prevents any blockage. But when you have three or four cards headed by an honour in partner's suit, lead your lowest card.

from   A 5 2   lead the two
        K 8 5   five
        Q 4 3   three
        J 8 6 4   four

Here the idea is to trap an intermediate honour card in the declarer's hand.

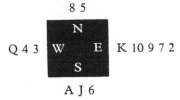

8 5

Q 4 3   K 10 9 7 2

A J 6

On your lead of the three, partner will play the king and the declarer the ace. When East eventually gains the lead he will be able to return the ten, trapping the jack and restricting South to one trick in the suit.

Note that South makes two tricks if you start by leading the queen.

Opening Leads Against Suit Contracts

There is little chance of establishing your long suit when the declarer has plenty of trumps. In defending against a suit contract, therefore, the emphasis is more on safety. You should try to find a lead that will not present the declarer with a cheap trick.

The difference in approach is most clearly seen when you have a holding such as A K 8 4 3. Against no trumps it is correct to lead the four, conceding an early trick in the hope of making four later tricks. Against a suit contract you cannot afford such generosity. The declarer may well have only two cards in the suit, and unless you score your ace and king on the first two rounds you will not score them at all. You should there-fore lead the king. This will give you a chance to look at dummy and plan the best continuation.

A lead from a sequence of three honour cards is both safe and con-structive.

A K̲ Q   K̲ Q J   Q̲ J 10   J̲ 10 9

When you have a broken sequence, or only two honours in sequence, there is an element of risk, but these leads are generally preferable to a lead from an unsupported honour card.

A K̲ 3   K̲ Q 10   Q̲ J 3   J̲ 10 5

You will note that the lead of the king can be ambiguous. However, partner will know that your king is supported by either the ace or the queen, and all uncertainty will be dispelled if he can see one of these cards in his own hand or in dummy.

When partner has bid a suit, lead your highest card from three small cards or from any doubleton, and your lowest from three or four cards headed by any honour except the ace. Lead the ace if you have it. After all, the declarer or dummy may have a singleton king.

Against a trump contract, never lead a low card from a suit headed by the ace. The danger of giving the declarer a trick that he cannot otherwise make is overwhelming. Try not to lead from holdings such as A 5 3, A Q 7 2, or A J 8 5, but if you must do so lead the ace.

Be wary also of leading away from lower honour cards. Any lead from an unsupported king, queen or jack may prove expensive.

8 3

K 10 7 4 2 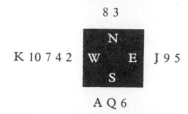 J 9 5

A Q 6

Here the declarer's queen is destined to be a loser, but it becomes a winner if you lead the suit from the West hand. At no trumps it may be worth while conceding an extra trick for the sake of establishing your long suit, but this consideration does not apply in a suit contract. All that the lead achieves is to throw away your natural trick in the suit.

Nevertheless, there are times when you have no option but to lead from an unsupported honour. The fourth-highest card (or the lowest of three) is then the right card to choose.

Short Suit Leads

A singleton lead, or the top card from a doubleton, may succeed in preparing the ground for a ruff. The best time to try it is when you have a fairly weak hand with three trumps headed by the ace or king. Partner is likely to have some cards of entry, and when you win your trump trick you can hope to put him in and get your ruff.

Trump Leads

A trump lead is the right choice when the bidding indicates that dummy's trumps will be used for ruffing.

	NORTH	SOUTH
♠: 9 3		
♡: 10 5 3		1 ♡
◇: K J 9 6	1 ♠	2 ◇
♣: A J 7 5	3 ♡	4 ♡

Your diamonds are well placed behind the declarer, but North, who has bid spades and supported hearts strongly, is likely to be short in diamonds. There is a danger that your diamond tricks may be ruffed away, and you should therefore aim to remove at least some of dummy's trumps. Lead the three of hearts.

Passive Leads

When no attractive lead is available, choose the lead that is least likely to cost a trick. This will often be a lead from three small cards.

NORTH   SOUTH

♠: 8 7 4
♡: K 7   1 ♡
◇: A Q 9 4   2 ♡   4 ♡
♣: Q 7 6 2

Here the safest lead is the eight of spades. Partner will recognize this as 'top of nothing' rather than 'fourth highest'.

Third Hand High

We now cross the table to consider the problems of the defender in the East seat. His first duty is to try to co-operate with his partner. The defenders will achieve nothing by pulling in different directions.

When partner leads a low card and there are only small cards in dummy, you should play your highest card in an attempt to win the trick. This will at least have the effect of forcing a higher card from the declarer's hand, thereby promoting your partner's cards.

7 2

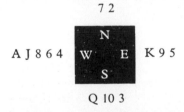

A J 8 6 4   K 9 5

Q 10 3

West leads the six against a no trump contract. Sitting East, you should play the king and return the nine. If you are too faint-hearted to play the king, the declarer will make an unexpected trick and his laughter will haunt your dreams.

8 6

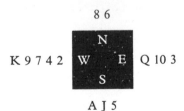

K 9 7 4 2   Q 10 3

A J 5

When West leads the four East should play the queen. This forces out the ace, and when East subsequently gains the lead he can return the ten, trapping the jack and picking up four tricks for the defence. Observe that if East fails to play the queen, South can win the first trick with the jack and still retain the ace to control the suit.

8 3

Q 9 7 5 2   A 10 4

K J 6

Similarly, when the five is led East must play the ace. Otherwise the declarer makes two tricks in the suit.

Lowest of Touching Cards

We have seen that in leading from a sequence of touching cards the highest card is chosen. This assures partner that the card immediately below is held as well.

In following suit, however, we give equally valuable information by playing the other way round. Holding two or three high cards in sequence, we play the lowest of the sequence.

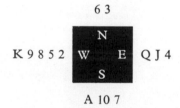

6 3

K 9 8 5 2   Q J 4

A 10 7

When West leads the five East still has a duty to play high. But touching cards are equals, in effect, and the jack is the right card to play. This helps to clarify the picture for West. When South wins the trick with the ace, West knows that his partner has the queen as well. It must be so, for the declarer would not have squandered the ace if he could have won with the queen. Consequently, when West regains the lead he has no qualms about leading a low card to his partner's queen.

When East fails to play the jack, the inference that the declarer has it is equally sure.

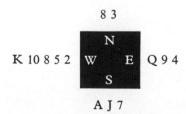

8 3

K 10 8 5 2   Q 9 4

A J 7

The five is led to the queen and ace. Knowing that East cannot have the jack, West will not be tempted to continue the suit when he regains

the lead. He will switch to another suit and wait for his partner to lead
through the jack.

The value of the information exchanged by the defenders can be seen
in the following hand.

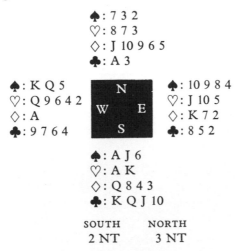

♠: 7 3 2
♡: 8 7 3
◇: J 10 9 6 5
♣: A 3

♠: K Q 5
♡: Q 9 6 4 2
◇: A
♣: 9 7 6 4

♠: 10 9 8 4
♡: J 10 5
◇: K 7 2
♣: 8 5 2

♠: A J 6
♡: A K
◇: Q 8 4 3
♣: K Q J 10

SOUTH	NORTH
2 NT	3 NT

West leads the four of hearts, East plays the ten and South wins with
the king. Needing to develop tricks in diamonds, the declarer leads his
jack of clubs to dummy's ace and returns the jack of diamonds. Looking
at the diamond sequence on the table, East sees that it would be point-
less to cover with the king. He plays low and West wins with the ace.
From the play to the first trick West knows that his partner has the jack
of hearts. If South had held the jack, he would have won the trick with
it rather than use his king. West therefore confidently leads the two of
hearts and South's second stopper is knocked out. East in turn knows
that his partner must have started with five hearts, since he led the four
originally and played the two on the next round. When he gains the lead
with the king of diamonds, therefore, East is not tempted to try his luck
in spades. He simply returns his heart to give his partner three
more tricks.

Thus on this hand the defenders win the race to establish their long suit
first. The advantage of the opening lead put them one step ahead, and
the declarer was not able to catch up.

Finesse Against Dummy's Honours

The third-hand-high maxim must not be followed slavishly when there are high cards in dummy. You should play only as high as is necessary in order to win the trick or to force a stopper from the declarer's hand.

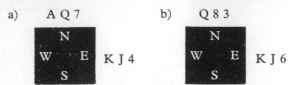

a) A Q 7   b) Q 8 3

W · E K J 4   W E K J 6

In diagram (a) when partner leads the suit and the seven is played from dummy, it is clearly unnecessary for you to play the king. The jack is high enough to win the trick. You can then switch to another suit, hoping to score a second trick with your king at a later stage.

Similarly, in diagram (b) it would be wasteful to play the king when partner leads and dummy plays low. The jack will either win the trick or force out the declarer's ace, and your king will be preserved for the important task of killing dummy's queen.
Here are some further examples.

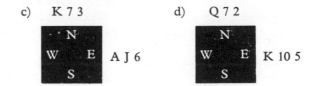

c) K 7 3   d) Q 7 2

W E A J 6   W E K 10 5

In each case West leads a small card and dummy plays low. The jack is the card to play in diagram (c). This will win the trick if partner has the queen. If the declarer has the queen, of course, he is bound to make a trick in the suit. And he will make two tricks if you play the ace.

In diagram (d) you should play the ten. This costs nothing, for if declarer has the jack he cannot be prevented from making a trick in the suit. If partner has the jack and declarer the ace, however, your ten will force out the ace and your king will eventually capture dummy's queen.

Unblocking

When partner leads an honour card from a sequence and you have a doubleton honour, it is important to avoid blocking the suit. Get rid of your honour card on the first round.

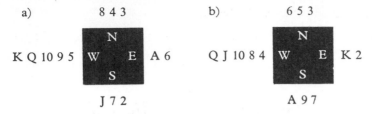

a) 8 4 3   b) 6 5 3

K Q 10 9 5   A 6   Q J 10 8 4   K 2

J 7 2   A 9 7

When West leads the king in diagram (a), East should overtake with the ace and return the six. The way is then clear for his partner to run the suit. If East plays low on the first round his ace will block the suit, and if West has no entry cards the suit will be dead.

Similarly, in diagram (b) East should play the king on his partner's lead of the queen. If he plays low, South may prevent the establishment of the suit either by winning the first trick with the ace and attacking West's entry or by holding up his ace for two rounds.

At first it may seem wasteful to play two high cards on the one trick, but you can usually afford the extravagance. When partner leads an honour card he promises several honours in sequence, so do not hesitate to get out of his way by playing your high cards. Unblocking is merely the technical term for the procedure of playing the high cards from the shorter holding first.

Returning Partner's Suit

After leading his long suit against a no trump contract, partner will expect you to return the suit when you gain the lead. Most of the time you should go along with his plan rather than launch a new attack of your own. At least it will keep partner's blood pressure down and make for an amiable game.

The question of which card to return is important. It is conventional to return your highest remaining card from an original holding of three, and the fourth-highest card from an original holding of four or more.

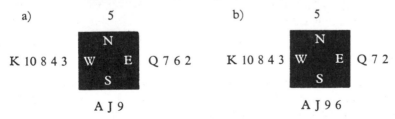

a) 5   b) 5

K 10 8 4 3   Q 7 6 2   K 10 8 4 3   Q 7 2

A J 9   A J 9 6

West leads the four and your queen is captured by the ace. In diagram (a) you return the two when you regain the lead. This tells West that you started with four cards in the suit, and on taking the nine with his ten he will continue with the king to drop the jack.

In diagram (b) your return of the seven gives partner an equally clear picture, telling him that South started with four cards in the suit. After winning the nine with his ten he will switch to another suit, hoping to put you back in to lead through the jack.

Let us have a look at a complete hand.

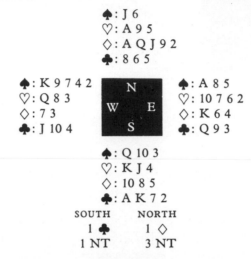

♠: J 6
♡: A 9 5
◊: A Q J 9 2
♣: 8 6 5

♠: K 9 7 4 2
♡: Q 8 3
◊: 7 3
♣: J 10 4

♠: A 8 5
♡: 10 7 6 2
◊: K 6 4
♣: Q 9 3

♠: Q 10 3
♡: K J 4
◊: 10 8 5
♣: A K 7 2

SOUTH	NORTH
1 ♣	1 ◊
1 NT	3 NT

West leads the four of spades against three no trumps. East wins with the ace and returns the eight, on which South trickily plays the queen. What should West do?

West can tell from his partner's return of the eight of spades that the declarer has the ten as well as the queen (with A 10 8 5 East would have returned the five). Hence it would not be good play for West to win this trick and continue with a third spade. Having no likely card of entry, he would then never have a chance to make his small spades.

The answer is to duck the second round of spades, playing the two instead of the king. The duck preserves the link between the East and West hands. When East gains the lead with the king of diamonds he returns his third spade to give West three more tricks in the suit.

Second Hand Low

In third position, as we have seen, it is right to play high in an attempt to win the trick. In second position, however, it is normally right to play low when a small card is led.

One reason is that if you are second to play your partner is fourth, and he may be able to win the trick more economically than you can. But the main reason is that it is seldom right to waste the power of a high card 'on air'. Aces should be preserved for capturing kings and queens, for in so doing they help to promote your intermediate cards. If all an ace catches is a two and a three, it is not being used to best advantage.

Consider this example.

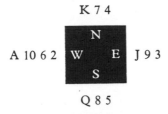

The declarer leads the five and makes two tricks in the suit if you play the ace. If you play low from the West hand he can make only one trick. The king cannot be prevented from winning, but your ace will eventually kill the declarer's queen.

When the declarer leads the five there is no reason for you to play the jack. South probably intends to play the ace from dummy anyway, and if he does not East is likely to be able to win the trick. If you are unwise enough to play the jack, South will win with dummy's ace and finesse the ten on the way back to make three tricks. He can make no more than two tricks if you play low.

Another good reason for playing low is to give the declarer a guess. Suppose this is a side suit in a trump contract and the declarer leads the five from dummy.

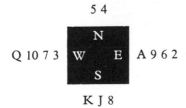

If East hops up with the ace he solves the declarer's problem. If East plays low without hesitation, the declarer may well do the wrong thing, finessing the jack and allowing the defenders to make two tricks in the suit.

Hold-Up in Defence

Although aces and kings are best employed in capturing queens and jacks, this does not mean that they should always do so at the first opportunity. This hand illustrates the value of a defensive hold-up.

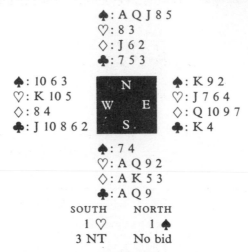

♠: A Q J 8 5
♡: 8 3
◇: J 6 2
♣: 7 5 3

♠: 10 6 3
♡: K 10 5
◇: 8 4
♣: J 10 8 6 2

♠: K 9 2
♡: J 7 6 4
◇: Q 10 9 7
♣: K 4

♠: 7 4
♡: A Q 9 2
◇: A K 5 3
♣: A Q 9

SOUTH	NORTH
1 ♡	1 ♠
3 NT	No bid

West leads the jack of clubs, on which East plays the king and South the ace. At trick two the declarer leads a spade and finesses dummy's jack.

First consider what happens if East wins the trick with the king. He can return his club to knock out the queen, but South makes two clubs, two diamonds, one heart and four spades for a total of nine tricks.

Observe the difference if East plays low on the first spade, allowing the jack to win. Now the declarer is unable to establish the spades for lack of an entry to dummy. He may return to hand with a diamond and repeat the spade finesse, but East takes his king on the second round and South is cut off from dummy. Even if South refuses to take a second spade finesse, he will make no more than eight tricks against careful defence.

Look out for opportunities of cutting communications by holding up your high cards in this way. They come along quite often.

Signals

You may feel an urge to smile and nod your head when you like your partner's lead, but you must restrain yourself. The laws of the game do not permit any display of approval or disapproval by word or gesture, requiring you to maintain an impassive manner at all times.

However, there is a perfectly legal equivalent of the smile and the nod. To show a liking for partner's lead, just play a card that is higher than necessary on the first round of the suit. The message is confirmed when you follow with a lower card on the second round. This high-low signal or 'echo' is one of the most useful tools of defence. Here is how it works.

                    9 6 4

          A K 5   Q 8 7 2

                    J 10 3

When West leads the king East plays the eight to call for a continuation. On the lead of the ace East completes his echo by playing the two, and the defenders take all their tricks in the suit.

Conversely, a defender plays his lowest card on the first round when he wishes to discourage his partner from continuing the suit.

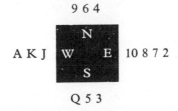

                    9 6 4

          A K J   10 8 7 2

                    Q 5 3

In this case, when West leads the king, East has no reason to ask for a continuation. He therefore plays the two, a highly discouraging card. West will switch to another suit, and later East may be able to lead through the declarer's queen.

When you concede a trick to the declarer your choice of card may again convey a message.

                    6 4 3

          10 5   A K 9 8 2

                    Q J 7

Defending against a no trump contract, partner leads the ten of your suit. If you lack an outside entry your correct play is to duck on the first round, but you should play the nine in order to encourage partner to continue the suit when he regains the lead.

When partner leads a king against a suit contract, start an echo if you have a doubleton. You will encounter this situation over and over again.

Q 9 2

A K 10 8 5   7 3

J 6 4

Encourage with the seven on the lead of the king. Partner will continue with the ace, and when your three appears he will know that you can ruff the third round.

Discard Signals

When you are unable to follow suit, try to guide your partner to the right defence by making an informative discard. The same principle holds good. The discard of a high card is a request for a lead of that suit, while the discard of a low card expresses lack of interest in the suit.

♠: A 7 6 3
♡: 8 6
◇: A 9 8 5 3
♣: 7 6

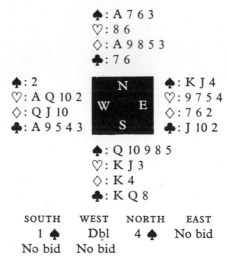

♠: 2   ♠: K J 4
♡: A Q 10 2   ♡: 9 7 5 4
◇: Q J 10   ◇: 7 6 2
♣: A 9 5 4 3   ♣: J 10 2

♠: Q 10 9 8 5
♡: K J 3
◇: K 4
♣: K Q 8

SOUTH	WEST	NORTH	EAST
1 ♠	Dbl	4 ♠	No bid
No bid	No bid		

West leads the queen of diamonds and the king wins the trick. The declarer leads a spade to the ace, and continues with a second spade which East wins with the king. On this trick West should discard the ten of hearts — the highest heart he can afford — to call for a heart switch.

Suppose that West's hearts had been A Q 3 2. The three of hearts is not high enough to act as a reliable messenger, and West would have had to make his point in a different way. By discarding the three of clubs, his lowest card in the suit, he could deny interest in clubs, and East would switch to a heart as before.

TIP FOR TODAY

Give partner all the help you
can. He is on your side.

13. Improving Your Game

Don't be alarmed by the heading. I am not proposing to launch you on a rigorous course of further study. You have learned the game with a view to having fun, after all, and if you want to stop reading and start enjoying yourself at this point it is all right with me. Having absorbed the contents of this book, you already know enough to play an intelligent game, and that is more than can be said for many bridge players.

However, bridge is a game that can give pleasure and satisfaction at many different levels. As your standard of play improves, the pleasure becomes more intense and the satisfaction more complete. A few words of advice for those who wish to make real progress may therefore not be out of place.

By definition, a beginners' book is limited in scope. We have examined only the basic structure of bidding and the fundamentals of play and defence. There is a great deal more to learn.

The bidding philosophy expounded in this book is that of the Acol system, which is by far the most popular bidding system in use in Britain today. Playing Acol, you can be sure of finding a like-minded partner in any corner of the country. As you widen your circle of bridge acquaintances, however, you will come into contact with other systems and with conventions which you have not met before. Do not be intimidated, and do not let anyone bully you into playing a convention that you do not fully understand. Tell your prospective partners that you play Acol with a strong no trump and Blackwood, and you will find that they will be happy to accommodate you. When you have had time to study some of the conventions that are new to you, you may decide to incorporate them in your methods.

You will also encounter advanced techniques in bidding and play from time to time. Do not be dismayed if the other players appear to know more about the game. As you gain experience you will gradually add to your knowledge, absorbing new ideas as soon as you are ready for them. The important thing is that you have a sound foundation on which to build.

Learn From Your Mistakes

It is rare for an expert to sit through a session of bridge without making a number of mistakes. As a beginner, you must expect to make between fifty and a hundred mistakes in the course of an evening's play. There is nothing shameful about this. It is only by making mistakes that you can gain the experience needed to improve your game. What you must try to avoid, however, is settling in a comfortable rut and committing the same errors over and over again. You can do this only by facing up to your errors and attempting to put a finger on the cause. When something goes wrong, either in the bidding or in the defence, make a point of discussing the matter with your partner after the game. If you can identify the bid or play that was responsible for the poor result, you will be half-way towards preventing a repetition. Don't be too ready to reproach your partner, for you will seldom be completely blameless yourself. The most rapid improvement is likely to be made by those who are willing to take most of the blame for a mishap on their own shoulders.

Bridge is so full of challenging mysteries that its allure can never fade. I have been playing the game for thirty years, yet I expect to learn something new every time I sit down at the table.

Choose Your Company

One of the quickest ways of improving your game is by playing as often as possible with better players. Do not stray too far out of your class, for that could be damaging both to your morale and to your wallet. But if you consistently seek the company of those whom you judge to be a little better than yourself, your progress should be rapid. Don't hesitate to ask advice about any points that may puzzle you. Most players will be delighted to help. At the same time, don't accept as gospel all the advice that is showered upon you. Many players have fixed ideas that are not altogether sound.

When you cannot raise a game, you may learn something by watching at an expert table. To get the most out of this exercise, position yourself behind one player so that you can see only his cards. Try to figure out the reasoning behind his bids and plays, and ask yourself if you would have taken the same action.

Further Reading

Bridge columns are featured in all the better national newspapers and in many local papers as well. These columns are written by the top international stars of the game and generally combine entertainment with a painless lesson on some aspect of bidding or play.

For those who like their bridge in larger doses there are many magazines devoted to the game. In Britain we have the old-established *Bridge Magazine*, published by John Waddington Ltd., Wakefield Road, Leeds, LS10 3TP. This is a monthly publication catering for players of all standards. Taking out an annual subscription would be a big step towards improving your game.

If you find it easy to learn from books you will not be hindered by lack of choice. Since contract bridge first began, many thousands of books have been written covering every facet of the game. On the market at the moment are a number of books capable of taking you on from the point where this one leaves you. Visit any good bookshop and take your pick.

A Word About Partners

Cet animal est très méchant,
Quand on l'attaque, il se défend.

A lesson that needs to be learned quickly is that all partners react unfavourably to criticism. Some tend to snap and snarl, others to brood and sulk. In either case the usual result is that the criticized partner makes a mess of the next hand as well as the last one. That costs you money, so it is in your own interest to avoid criticizing your partner between hands. If you can find something to congratulate him about, so much the better. A pat on the back may encourage him to play above himself.

As for partners who criticize you, well, you must try to put up with them. A thick skin is an asset while you are learning the game. Draw your partner's fangs by apologizing profusely for the error, consoling yourself with the reflection that he may know more about bridge, but that you are the better psychologist. If you can keep cool in the face of severe provocation, you have the makings of a player in a million.

TIP FOR EVERY DAY

Enjoy your bridge, win or lose.

Scoring Table

Below the Line

Trick Score

For each trick over six bid and made	UNDOUBLED	DOUBLED	REDOUBLED
In clubs or diamonds	20	40	80
In hearts or spades	30	60	120
In no trumps (first trick)	40	80	160
(each subsequent trick)	30	60	120

The first side to score 100 points below the line wins a game and is said to be vulnerable. Both sides start from scratch for the next game. The first side to win two games wins the rubber.

Above the Line

Bonuses

For honours in one hand	
All five trump honours, or four aces at no trumps	150
Four trump honours	100

For bidding and making a slam	NOT VULNERABLE	VULNERABLE
Small slam (12 tricks)	500	750
Grand slam (13 tricks)	1000	1500

For winning the rubber		Unfinished rubber	
In two games	700	One game in unfinished rubber	300
In three games	500	A part-score in unfinished game	50

For making any doubled or redoubled contract	50

Overtricks

For each overtrick made:	UNDOUBLED	DOUBLED	REDOUBLED
Not vulnerable	Trick value	100	200
Vulnerable	Trick value	200	400

Undertricks
Penalties scored by defenders when declarer falls short of contract.

	UNDOUBLED	DOUBLED		REDOUBLED	
	Each Trick	First Trick	Subsequent Tricks	First Trick	Subsequent Tricks
Not vulnerable	50	100	200	200	400
Vulnerable	100	200	300	400	600